PRAISE FOR
BEAUTY RESTORED

What encouragement! *Beauty Restored* reveals a God who knows
all our pain and sorrow and hopelessness. Me Ra Koh's own
testimony shows that God not only knows but also that He cares,
He is able, and He is big enough to rescue us and to heal our souls
from every affliction. *Beauty Restored* offers all of us this hope.

Audrey Alman
WASHINGTON STATE DIRECTOR, MARRIAGE MINISTRIES INTERNATIONAL

This book is a reminder and encouragement to the Church
and nonbelievers alike that God desires to set people free from
the chains of injustice.

Ché Ahn
SENIOR PASTOR, HARVEST ROCK CHURCH

Me Ra Koh takes us on a sacred journey—a riveting, honest,
intimate and wise story of hope and healing. No matter what your
hurt, you will find in these pages a friend sent from God to
validate your process of healing.

Janet M. Congo
COFOUNDER, LIFEMATES MINISTRIES

Beauty Restored is a long overdue work, thoughtfully and sensitively written. Me Ra Koh has opened her heart to us and revisited pain largely ignored by the Church and only whispered elsewhere. With this book she has given a priceless gift of hope and direction to a culture that desperately needs it. Thank you, Me Ra!

Roger Hillerstrom
AUTHOR OF *INTIMATE DECEPTION*

If you are a victim of date rape, *Beauty Restored* is essential reading. You know the trauma of being horribly violated—and so does Me Ra Koh. Her courageous story will inspire you and give you the hope she found along her path to healing.

Les and Leslie Parrott
AUTHORS OF *RELATIONSHIPS*

Me Ra Koh courageously invites the reader along on her personal journey of healing. She articulately and honestly describes the betrayal, fear, isolation and extreme depth of pain experienced by a recovering victim. Yet a look into her soul also exposes the path to God's light, truth and ultimate freedom. You will find hope and valuable help within these pages, as will anyone who has suffered so profoundly as to feel abandoned by God.

Kay Scott
AUTHOR OF *SEXUAL ASSAULT: WILL I EVER FEEL OKAY AGAIN?*

In writing this powerful testimony, Me Ra Koh has taken a bold and courageous step that will have a great impact on many lives and perhaps save many as well. Once again for the child of God, what the enemy meant for evil, God has used for good.

Wendell and Gini Smith
SENIOR PASTORS, THE CITY CHURCH
KIRKLAND, WASHINGTON

Beauty Restored is a book for victims, their families and friends, and for ministers and counselors. Me Ra Koh offers hope and important information for each of us. I will have my teenagers read this book.

Debra Taylor
AUTHOR OF *SECRETS OF EVE*

For those who have known the trauma of rape and for all those who desire to help them, Me Ra Koh's story is a poignant, courageous testimony of how the power of God will prevail when He is invited to become not only Savior but also Lord.

Barbara Wright
ASSOCIATE PASTOR, THE CITY CHURCH
KIRKLAND, WASHINGTON

$\mathcal{B}$eauty restored

Me Ra Koh

Regal

A Division of Gospel Light
Ventura, California, U.S.A.

Published by Regal Books
A Division of Gospel Light
Ventura, California, U.S.A.
Printed in the U.S.A.

Regal Books is a ministry of Gospel Light, an evangelical Christian publisher dedicated to serving the local church. We believe God's vision for Gospel Light is to provide church leaders with biblical, user-friendly materials that will help them evangelize, disciple and minister to children, youth and families.

It is our prayer that this Regal book will help you discover biblical truth for your own life and help you meet the needs of others. May God richly bless you.

For a free catalog of resources from Regal Books/Gospel Light, please call your Christian supplier or contact us at 1-800-4-GOSPEL *or* www.regalbooks.com.

Cover and interior design by Robert Williams
Edited by Deena Davis

Library of Congress Cataloging-in-Publication Data
Koh, Me Ra, 1973-
    Beauty restored / Me Ra Koh.
        p. cm.
    Includes bibliographical references (p.).
    ISBN 0-8307-2761-2
    1. Koh, Me Ra, 1973- 2. Acquaintance rape victims—Religious life. 3. Acquaintance rape—Religious aspects—Christianity. I. Title.

BV4596.A3 .K64 2001
261.8'3272—dc21   00-051837

1 2 3 4 5 6 7 8 9 10 11 12 13 14 15 / 09 08 07 06 05 04 03 02 01

Rights for publishing this book in other languages are contracted by Gospel Literature International (GLINT). GLINT also provides technical help for the adaptation, translation and publishing of Bible study resources and books in scores of languages worldwide. For further information, contact GLINT, P.O. Box 4060, Ontario, CA 91761-1003, U.S.A. You may also send e-mail to Glintint@aol.com, or visit their website at www.glint.org.

Though you have made me see troubles, many and bitter,
you will restore my life again.

PSALM 71:20

She left pieces of her life behind her everywhere she went. "It's easier
to feel the sunlight without them," she said.

BRIAN ANDREAS
Still Mostly True: Collected Stories and Drawings

Dedicated to Four Beautiful Women

Emma, Lynne and Taylor

When I had nothing, you took me in your arms
and breathed life, laughter and loveliness into my soul.
I am forever grateful.

My mom

When I am a mother, I want to love my children the way you do.
I wouldn't be here if you hadn't heard my cry for help.
Thank you.

Contents

Part One
Hiding in Dark Places

Part Two
Moving from Depression to Grief

Part Three
Stepping into the Light

Appendix One
How Others Viewed My Journey to Healing

Appendix Two
Resources for Rape Victims and Those Who Want to Help Them

Foreword

Date rape is not difficult to define if you have been a victim of it. Sex that is forced upon you in any form feels like rape whether it is from someone you know or someone you have never met. No matter who the perpetrator is, the sense of loss, violation, shame and fear are the same.

There is absolutely no circumstance, no scenario, that justifies taking something sacred from a person. There is no rationalization, no assumed provocation, that can justify doing such harm to one of God's great and wonderful creations. If a man stole from his date, could he justify it by saying she had too much money in her purse? The only reason a woman is raped is because a man is out of control, sick and saturated with sin.

If you have been date raped, you may have been convinced you asked for it or even deserved it. That is not true. No one deserves or asks for rape. That is why it is called rape. You are not responsible for the cruel act committed against you. What you are responsible for is healing and somehow forgiving so that you can move on beyond the heinous crime.

Exercising forgiveness does not mean you are justifying what happened or excusing it. Forgiveness does not change the nature of the crime, but it allows you to move on, free from the horror and free to start a new life absent of shame and regret.

In these pages, Me Ra Koh offers her own story with great dignity, vulnerability and hope. The very act of admitting what happened and offering understanding to others proclaims that her pain and grief was not in vain. In writing about her tragedy and the difficult process of recovery, she leads those who have gone through a similar experience to the promised land of hope and health, where they can once again find a way to be close to God and to trust Him, even though they have discovered how untrustworthy His creations can be.

Read this book with anticipation. Follow Me Ra's lead so that you no longer live as a victim but as someone who has experienced victory over the inhumane act of another. Allow God to strengthen you and to perform the same miracle in your life.

Now a word to men: I pray that you will spend the time needed to read this book. It will introduce you to a real human being— a real woman with real feelings. You may discover thoughts and feelings within yourself that you never knew existed. I hope that before you finish reading, you will realize for the first time the depth and magnitude of the crimes of rape and sexual assault.

The appetite of a man, when it is out of control, wreaks destruction on all those around him. Even so, it is never too late to undo the damage and rebuild the landscape of a human life. The most amazing news for those who have taken part in this crime is that God wants to see you move beyond this. God wants you to accept His forgiveness, and He wants you to forgive yourself so that you are free from the compulsions that might lead you back into this despicable act.

To those who have never been raped, this book is still for you. All you have to do is fill in the source of your pain and Me Ra's story will show you the path toward true and lasting healing. The path she chose is an example of what God can do when you choose not to use Him as an excuse for what someone has done to you. Me Ra is proof that what was meant for evil can be used to release captives from their bondages of abuse and victimization.

Please read this book thoughtfully and attentively, and then pass on what you have learned to others who need to know that God has been there for them all the time. However you came upon this great work of vulnerability, I pray that you will respond to it and become a person who is honored by our Lord for the dramatic changes you have sought in your life and allowed Him to bring about.

Stephen Arterburn
Founder of New Life Clinics

Preface

―~―

Dear Reader,

If you have been date raped, I invite you to come with me on a journey of restoration. You will read about my own journey toward healing and, I hope, find comfort for your pain or the pain of someone you love.

When I was just starting out on my path to recovery, I held on to a slim thread of hope that God could do better than just help me put the rape behind me. I didn't want only survival; I wanted life—my life—back. You probably feel that way too. Although I don't have any easy answers, I've seen a lot, cried a lot and, over time, have been transformed. Eventually, that slim thread of hope became a strong cord that pulled me from darkness into light. I want to offer that same hope to you.

The dream behind this project was to let other date rape victims know that they are not alone. You now hold that dream in your hands. My desire is that each of you will take the time to sit in safety with a book that puts into words the breadth and depth of your own pain. I want you to be able to follow Jesus through the darkness and devastating hurt and enter the light once again.

The Lord extends His hand to us for healing. But it is the kind of healing that feels like death, even as it brings restoration. I want you to see that you are meant to be more than a survivor of date rape. You are invited to be an overcomer.

Now let me explain what this book is not. It is not a self-help book. You will not find three easy steps to a better life here. Instead, this book shares the reality of pain. Some pain goes so deep that we can only express it through story or allegory. You will find sections of allegory throughout these pages. I have also chosen to tell about the death of my friend Alex because of the impact his life and death had on me. As a victim of date rape, I grieved many "deaths": the loss of innocence, the loss of my virginity, the loss of joy and more. The trauma of Alex's death only compounded the losses.

Although I wrote this book for victims of date rape, people who helped with the development of the manuscript shared that they were touched. Pain seems to bring all sufferers to a common ground. After the death of his wife, Christian apologist and author C. S. Lewis wrote the following about God:

> [You] go to Him when your need is desperate, when all other help is vain, and what do you find? A door slammed in your face, and a sound of bolting and double bolting on the inside. After that, silence.*

Pain often makes us feel as if God has left us. The journey of healing asks us to walk a road that feels like the valley of death. Yet this road is actually the path of hope. I open my journey to you because even though I, too, felt abandoned by God, He never let go of me.

Your path to freedom may be more difficult—or less difficult—than mine. Whatever your path may bring, I share my story with you so that you might have hope.

Gentle blessings,
Me Ra Koh

* C. S. Lewis, *A Grief Observed* (New York: Bantam Books, 1961), p. 4.

A Special Note to Men Who Read This Book

~

Although most date rape victims are women, the crime of rape also happens to men. Pain is pain, regardless of gender.

I wrote this book for a feminine audience; but as the book drew near completion, I felt the Lord impress upon me that the message should not be limited to women.

Some of the men who were asked to read the manuscript before the book was published had been raped or sexually abused. It was an honor to know that the words of this book brought them comfort and eased their pain.

If you are a man reading this book, please accept this word of validation of your painful experiences. I invite you to come along on the journey to restoration; and I pray that you will find comfort, healing and hope. May God bless you on your road to freedom.

Respectfully,
Me Ra Koh

Acknowledgments

I have heard that writing your first book is like giving birth to a baby. This "baby" will have been in development for nine years by the time it finally hits the bookstores. To give birth to this precious book meant letting others into some of the most intimate places of my hurt and struggles. I could not have done it and still be doing it without a community of people who saw hope and truth in my story—these are the people who must be recognized.

- I went to Linda Wagner nine years ago and asked her how to write a book. She exhorted me to start writing whatever came out of my heart. In many ways, she has been the driving force behind this project. She believed in me and the book every step of the way. I thank you, Linda Wagner, of Lindeberg Literary Services, for your amazing project development, gracious and faithful author support, and committed marketing work. May your life be blessed a hundredfold for all you have sown into mine.
- Special thanks to all the "guinea pigs" who read drafts of this book when they were in their roughest stages: Tammy Perron, Glen Vanderwerff, Heather and Jason Needham, John Chase, Kathi Allen (thank you also for your help with the book proposal), Linda Wagner's critique group, and many other people I have never even met. You know who you are, and I am deeply grateful to you.

- Thank you, Pastor Ché Ahn, for introducing me to Regal Books. That was a divine appointment!
- Regal Books has been the most delightful and wonderfully supportive publisher to work with. Kyle Duncan and Bill Greig III, thank you for taking a risk on this book and believing in this ministry. Thank you, David Webb, Kim Bangs, Deena Davis, Marlene Baer and the rest of the team at Regal Books for making this the best book possible.
- Thank you to Pastor Ed and Carolyn Cook and the family at Seattle Vineyard Christian Fellowship. I went up for prayer every Sunday morning and evening for two years and never felt that any of you tired of me. Thank you for your ministry to my broken heart.
- My thanks to Pastor Wendell and Gini Smith and the family at The City Church. Your faith and exhoration continues to take me to new levels.
- I will always be grateful to Stephen Arterburn, founder of New Life Clinics, for coming to my college. Would I still be alive if God hadn't sent you to my school when He did? Thank you.
- I must also acknowledge the wonderful team of counselors who worked with me at New Life Clinics. You took me in when I was at my lowest point. Through your help and counsel the Lord began to breathe life back into me. If I hadn't gone to your clinic, there might not have been a book. If any of my fellow patients stumble upon this book, I just want to say, "We did it! We faced our stuff, and we made it." I'll never forget any of you and how you shared your lives with me.

- Roger Hillerstrom and Christine Ganfield are two others who helped me find wholeness through their gift of counseling. Thank you for holding my hand on those days I was afraid to move forward.
- Thank you, Rose Reynoldson, for your unending prayers for me, beginning nine years ago. And a thank-you to all the others who have covered me and this book in constant prayer.
- Thanks to my dear friends Leif and Anna Hansen, Chris and Shalom Shreve, and John Louviere. I will always treasure our days together when we ran after God and didn't ever think to slow down, no matter how early in the morning it was—smile.
- Thank you, Spike and Marilyn Scherrer, for opening your home to me. Thank you for our talks in the library at night (I always loved the things I learned form those evenings), for your constant love and for your rose garden.
- I also want to express my thankfulness to all the women reading this book who have been sexually violated. This book is a tribute to you. May you not feel alone in your journey to complete restoration.

There is one last group that is of the utmost importance. To put into print a painful part of life that sometimes you would rather forget takes the support of those who live with you day in, day out. Their support is vital because they in some ways choose to live with the pain of this subject as well.

- Ahba, my daddy, thank you for not being ashamed of your little girl. Thank you for reading every word of this book, no matter how much it hurt you to read them. Thank you for believing me.

- Mom, thank you for allowing me to be who I am, even when it means that I share the hard things. You are my role model in so many ways. I look to you when I want to know what it means to be a woman of God.

- Shae Min and Shaunie, my little brothers, thank you for loving your sister through a difficult time. Thank you for being proud of me now.

- To my extended family of grandparents, in-laws, uncles, aunts and cousins, thank you for seeing me as me. I hold your support and love as gifts in my life.

- And most important of all, thank you, my dear husband, Brian. How can I sum up my gratitude for your life in one paragraph? No matter what I say it will not come close to all that you have sacrificed. You have given your life to me by blessing this book and my vulnerability. You have chosen to always live with this story. You have worked longer hours day after day, so I could be writing at home. You are my comfort in the middle of the night when an old nightmare returns. You see a woman of faith in me when I only see insecurity and brokenness. You are the husband I never thought I was worthy enough to have, and yet I know I am worthy when I am with you. You are my soulmate, my best friend.

Part One

Hiding in Dark Places

Lord, my heart aches deeply and the loneliness

is beginning to consume me. I cry out in the dark.

Lord, will You answer?

MY JOURNAL ENTRY

Chapter One

Hidden in Shame

—~—

The United States Department of Justice reports that
someone is raped once every five minutes.

CRIME IN THE UNITED STATES, 1991

It was a small Christian college. Freshman orientation had just
begun. My mom and my aunt had helped me move into my
dorm room and had now left for home.

It was early evening and I was in line for the barbecue dinner.
He was in front of me. I remember that his jokes made everyone
around him laugh. Then he turned around and started a conversation with me. He seemed nice; but as we talked, there were
things I did not understand: He was not a freshman, he was an
older student taking time off from school. He was not helping
out with the orientation activities, he was simply there to meet
the incoming freshmen. I wondered about these things, but
I laid my questions aside.

He was fun to be with and he made me laugh—it wasn't hard to be his friend. Within a month we were dating. I felt flattered that a Christian man was noticing me and pursuing me. He said I was beautiful and that he loved me. He sent me huge bouquets of fragrant flowers. He bought me cards and wrote Scriptures mixed with confessions of his love. My heart wanted to believe him. At the same time, I now realize that I was blinding myself to how he was slowly changing.

When we first started dating, he loved everything about me. He loved the way I dressed, the way I laughed, the way I interacted with my girlfriends, the way I loved God. But this was only a façade.

At first he picked on small things; as time went on, his dissatisfaction with me and my world grew. One day he decided he didn't like my roommate, so I distanced myself from her. One night he didn't like the outfit I was going to wear to dinner, so I changed. Another night he mocked the way I had applied my makeup and said it was ugly to him. I went to the bathroom and stared at myself in the mirror, wondering if I had applied too much makeup.

When we went out to eat, he would smile at other women and give them attention. He disregarded how I felt about it. Instead, he would tell me what he liked about them and what I was lacking. I remember one incident in particular. We were waiting to be seated for dinner. A woman in a red business suit was sitting at a table nearby. Her legs were crossed. He complimented her long legs and then looked at mine.

How could he say my legs weren't good enough? How could I change my legs? Something inside me surrendered. Instead of trying to change everything about myself to please him, I began hoping that I was good enough for him to love.

After five long months of a bad relationship only getting worse, I decided I had to end the relationship. When I finally got up the courage to call things off, he got angry. He felt the Lord was telling him we were to be married. I felt confused. I wondered if God was disappointed with my trying to break up a relationship He had planned. I went to my girlfriends for support and realized I had given them up months ago to please him. My friends loved me, but I felt out of the loop of their love. I felt alone.

A few weeks later, he called and invited me out for dinner (as friends). We decided to go on Valentine's Day night. Dinner was awful. He treated me with little respect and I could tell I wasn't the only one who was disgusted. The waiters and the people at surrounding tables noticed his obnoxious yet so-called cool behavior.

We had used my car because he was temporarily without one. When he asked to drive back to the dorm, I didn't think anything of it. I was more than ready for the evening to end. Unfortunately, he hadn't intended to drive me home—yet. He had planned to take me to a deserted parking lot.

I remember very few things about the night I was raped. I can barely see the car windshield covered with fog. I can feel the struggle and I can see the moment I decided to give up. In that moment, I realized there was nothing I could do to prevent what was happening. Even though I struggled, he was too strong. He was overpowering. He was someone I had trusted, but now he was a monster. A demon in the flesh. What was I? Helpless.

The moment I realized I was helpless, I had to leave emotionally. My mind and feelings traveled to a distant land. I was looking for refuge within myself while my outward self was being stripped of all dignity. If I could find a place to hide, then maybe I could survive the rape. My heart was running . . . searching. It wanted to go as far away from reality as possible. My heart did find places—hidden places.

When it was over, he took me back to my dorm and told me he would give me a call. I was in shock. All I remember about those hours immediately after the rape was crying under the showerhead with all my clothes on.

The week afterward has always been foggy to me. I remember calling my mom and telling her what had happened. "I've been raped, Mom. I've been raped. I'm so sorry."

I could hear her fight back the tears. It broke her heart to hear the news. My father didn't know how to handle it. I was his only daughter, so he chose not to acknowledge what had happened. We were all in shock.

I felt desperate for hope, help, love and understanding. But people avoid saying the word "rape," because they think it helps you. That avoidance only made me feel more ashamed. The shock of the rape also brought to the surface painful memories of other areas of insecurity. I've since learned that I am not alone in this experience. Rape, especially acquaintance or date rape— which is a betrayal of trust—can expose other areas of hurt or vulnerability in your life. The result is a pain that goes deeper than anyone can imagine.

I wanted the pain to go away, so I attempted going through counseling. I remember having difficulty putting my feelings into words. Often the counselor would sit in her leather chair and I would sit on the leather couch across from her. I would hold my cup of tea and wonder why I'd even come to the session. How could I get better if all I felt was darkness?

One day she said to me, "Me Ra, if you could describe your heart's state as a place, what would that place look like?" My mouth couldn't articulate my anger, bitterness and disappointment, but it could tell her a story—in an allegory—about what the place my spirit was living in looked like. It was a place where pictures of the mind strain to describe the pain inside the heart.

My heart is like a dungeon. It is an empty, barren room. I can't see anything. There is no light. It is damp and filled with an aroma of mold. I live here. Alone. Lonely? Yes. Afraid? Always. Hopeful? No. This is my heart—a room of shame.

So much time has gone by that I have forgotten what light feels like. I cannot even remember what it looks like. Darkness befriends me; and although I don't enjoy its company, it is all I feel worthy of. This place reflects me. This is where I belong.

All hearts have doors and so does mine. My heart's door is made of heavy concrete. At the top of the door is a small window. When you glance up, you can barely see the silhouettes of people passing by. You could call this light, but to me light has to be more than a silhouette. Light is all-encompassing, isn't it?

No one dares to enter this dungeon. They can smell the mold. They can tell it is filthy here. I don't think they believe that someone could exist in this room. Yet here I am, living in this darkness. If anyone does see me, I am mistaken for dead. But I am breathing—ever so slowly. Somewhere in this dark room I am alive.

How will anyone ever find me here and why would anyone want to venture into this prison? Shame fills my heart with hopelessness. Shame is thrown at me like clumps of black clay. It smudges the walls of my heart. When people see the amount of shame in this cell, they turn their heads. It is much easier for people to look in and then pass by, ignoring the fact that this place of shame even exists. Maybe some of them look in and are glad they do not live within its walls. Who could blame them?

A face stares through the window. He is wearing a hooded cloak. I can't tell who he is. I want him to go away. I can't understand why so many people enjoy seeing others suffer. Why is my pain such an entertainment to others? Don't they know their staring eyes pierce my heart like cold spikes?

I look back at the window; his silhouette is gone. Secretly I wish he would have ventured in and pulled me out of this place.

Then I hear the hinges on the door begin to squeak. The handle is being rattled from the other side. I can hear the groans of a man pushing against the door with all his strength. I shrink into the corner of the room, trying to hide behind the darkness. The door opens and he comes in.

"Hello," he whispers.

Silence.

"Are you in here, Me Ra?" he asks.

How does this man know my name? I want to scream and shout "Here I am! I am here!" But I lie silent. I am too afraid. Still, I utter a silent prayer: *If he is a good man, don't take him away. Let him stay. Don't let him give up. Let him see that I'm alive and worth saving.*

I see his body turn. His hands grope the walls. The blackness of shame covers his palms. He falls to his knees and begins to weep. Then he rips off his cloak and exposes his flawless, clean body to the filth of this place. I want to scream "No, cover yourself from this filth! What are you doing? You're making a mistake!"

The sound of his weeping rings through me like the cry of a bell. "Father," he cries. "Why has my child lived in this place? Grace and mercy, come now and fill this room with your gentle comfort. Father, I plead for her life."

Months have passed since the first day he entered. I still live in the same room, but he is living with me. He sings songs of comfort and peace to me. Every day he tells me the story of his search for me. He wanted his little girl back. He wanted me.

For a long time I couldn't believe this. Days passed and I continued to lie still, like death. I thought if I looked dead, he would give up and leave. I wanted him to realize that I'm not who he thinks I am. I'm worthless. He's made a mistake. I knew he would eventually realize this and go away.

But he didn't. Instead, he continued to softly sing and gently wipe my brow and say prayers of healing over me. He believed in my life. He believed that I was worth saving. He was my Father. The Father of that all-encompassing light.

My counselor saw hope in the place I described. You might think I could have recognized the same hope. But it wasn't until years later that I finally saw that there actually was life in that dark room. All I knew then was the pain of shame.

As many of you have experienced, people are at a loss to know how to help you through pain that feels hopelessly endless. When people catch a glimpse of how deep your wounds go, they may feel overwhelmed. This is not bad. It isn't their fault that they can't understand. And yet I needed someone who could understand. I needed someone who could sit through all my tears. There is only one person who can do this. His name is God. He calls Himself Jesus.

Maybe you know Him well or, possibly, not well at all. Either way, you may feel some of what I felt. In the beginning, even though I knew enough of God to believe He could take away the filthiness I felt inside, I was afraid to let Him help me. I didn't want to see a bright light burst into my darkness. A shining knight couldn't save me. I wanted and needed something different.

Why did I feel this way? Because pain was all I had left. I couldn't let it go freely unless I knew the hands that took my pain were hands that understood. I needed to know that God felt my pain before He took it all away. I wanted God to sit in my pit of filth and cry with me. Inside, I was wasting away. I needed someone to name my pain and love me out of it.

When something traumatic like rape happens, one of the first questions the victim asks God is, Where were You if You really loved me? It is a question that cries out from the deepest part of our pain. I asked this question, and many others, countless times. It seemed like I had entered a dark room where time stood still. In my bitter resentment, I challenged Christ to reveal His so-called love. I was desperate for truth. I was desperate for a new beginning. And He gently answered. His answer was one word—Jesus. Jesus loved me back to life.

How? He sat in my darkness with me and took it on Himself. He spoon-fed me life. He saw my state of death and was not overwhelmed. Never once did He say, "Me Ra, you know it isn't that bad. A rape can't hurt this much, especially a date rape. You can get up, Me Ra. You can live if you would just try harder." Never did He say these things. He was content to sit in my pain. He was content to be with me. He knew that pain separates us from people. He knew that I had been separated and felt alone. He knew that I felt ashamed of who I was and what the rape had done to me.

Jesus gently came and sat in my ugliness. I felt His tears hit my face, and I began to realize I was the one He was crying for. My pain affected Him deeply. My pain caused His heart to cry out to the Father for life—new life.

As God's children, we are all healed in different ways. I believe that each healing is a gift from our Father. Each healing is also unique to the cry of our individual hearts. The cry of my heart was to know the God who would enter my shame, sit in my pain and cry with me.

He cried for me when I didn't have enough life to cry for myself. I saw His anger and watched His heart break when I told Him how much of me the rape had destroyed. I saw His love. And at some mysterious point, I began to believe.

Chapter Two

Finding My Voice

———~———

I said to my soul, be still, and let the dark come upon you
which shall be the darkness of God. As, in a theatre, the lights are
extinguished, for the scene to be changed.

T. S. ELIOT, *FOUR QUARTETS*,
"EAST COKER," III

I was told that the process of going through the court system
would feel like being raped a second time, but I didn't believe anything could be as bad as being trapped in that car. I was wrong.

I reported the rape in the summer of 1992 and we began the
process of filing charges. We started by applying for a restraining order. If we won round one, we would continue to press our
case. Months later, on a cold fall morning, I stood before a
woman judge and was asked, "Why didn't you scream or even
yell? Why didn't you just get out of the car? And why didn't you
fight harder?"

The lawyer's questions were worse. He practically snarled the words, "If this really happened, why aren't you crying?"

I began to sob.

"See?" the lawyer said. "I present to the judge a broken woman who is obviously emotionally unstable." He rested his case.

I couldn't win. If I cried, I looked like a weak woman who didn't know right from left. If I didn't cry, the lawyer questioned my story because I showed no emotional trauma. The lawyer for the man who raped me twisted everything I said and found a way to turn my words against me. I had to repeat the story so many times that I started to get confused. I felt overwhelmed. A whole courtroom of people heard every detail of the rape. Intimate parts of me were being "proven" filthy and dirty. I was being raped a second time.

I had asked my mom to stand outside the courtroom. I didn't want her to hear the details of what had happened that night. I asked my friend Alex to sit in the back. Alex was like a brother to me and was someone I had met through church. He had been sexually abused as a child and could relate to my pain. He supported me for standing up for what was right. Since I had been wounded by a Christian man, I saw Alex's friendship as a gift from God. He was a man around whom I actually felt safe.

The man I was charging with rape had invited his parents, his aunts and uncles and his pastor to the hearing. I'll never forget the look in some of their eyes. They hated me. I knew they didn't understand. But how had I, the victim, become the enemy?

I remember seeing Alex's face in the audience. I could tell he was trying not to cry. He slowly shook his head and looked at his shoes. He was ashamed of the injustice. I looked toward the doors at the entrance to the courtroom and saw my mom looking through the glass window. She was crying. The look on her face is one of the most painful memories of that time. It was one thing for me to go through the pain; it was another to watch her suffer too.

The verdict was announced. "Innocent . . . restraining order denied. Insufficient evidence."

I remember leaving the courtroom feeling completely drained. I wanted to collapse. I felt like a little girl who was scared and wanted her daddy to tell her everything was going to be all right. But it wouldn't be all right for a long time. I had just begun the painful process of healing.

I remember feeling like two different people inside. The woman in me had stood up for herself. She had been brave and courageous. She had stood her ground and watched her dignity deteriorate before her eyes. And now that it was over, the woman began to feel like a little girl who needed to be taken care of.

Months later, I wrote a story. It is a description of what was happening inside me. On the outside was a doubting lawyer, an unbelieving judge, my grieving mom and my being denied a restraining order.

On the inside, change was happening. I was a young woman—almost 20 years old. But at the same time, I was a child living in an adult body. For the first time, the woman in me heard the cry of the child and began to comfort her. The child was completely terrified. She wanted to curl up with her teddy bear and hide in a corner. She didn't want to go to court; she wanted to forget everything connected with the rape. The child needed the woman to stand up and say no. But I hadn't really been a woman before this time, so how could the little girl know that she would now be heard and protected?

I did stand up for myself in court. I said, "No, you can't do this. It is wrong, and you can't get away with it." The injustice of the verdict was a horrible loss. But the woman in me won something that day that I will never trade: She won her voice. The woman in me was beginning to build trust with the child by listening to her needs.

Sometimes we concentrate only on building trust with God. I found there was another relationship that needed nurturing. Before I could become a woman, the child in me needed to know she was safe and would always be heard.

I have listened to many stories and met many people who were sexually abused in their childhood or adolescent years. When the child tried to tell someone, no one listened. As the child became older, she stopped listening to that cry within her. Yet the little girl was still alive, scared and wondering if anyone would ever hear her. When I finally stopped and asked God for the courage to listen to the little girl's cry within me, this is what I heard.

Every day I sit alone at the window. I am scared and lonely and I wonder if there is anyone who can comfort me. I squeeze my teddy bear tightly. As I look out the window, I wonder what it is I'm looking for. For a hero? For someone to come and take me away from this room of pain? Or is my heart so tired that I'm dazed, just sitting, wanting and expecting nothing?

It's cold in this empty and plain room. There's nothing special to see and nothing special to gain. I want someone to play with or talk to, but who would that be? Who would want to enter this dark room? My teddy bear sits with me and loves me. But today even he isn't talkative. He, too, stares out the window.

"Teddy, do you see something?" I ask.

He doesn't answer. He doesn't like it here, and he tells me secrets about our running away together. But shhh! If anyone ever knew, we would be in big trouble. Teddy says it's not safe here and he doesn't like to see me cry so much. I tell him it's not that bad and we would be hurt more if we ever left.

The rain begins to sprinkle outside. I yawn and snuggle my head into Teddy's soft neck. Hours pass by and Teddy wakes to a quiet knock at the door. He quickly jumps in front of me to protect me from any bad person.

Then comes a voice.

"Me Ra, can I come in?"

I don't know whose voice it is. It sounds gentle and a little familiar, but I don't recognize it completely. Slowly the door opens and a woman wearing a black dress comes dancing into the room.

I bury my head in Teddy's stomach. He watches the woman for me and says she is beautiful. Her feet glide gently across the room. He says her smile makes him feel safe. He says she watches me as she dances.

I don't want her to know I care to meet her. But I have to see this woman. I take a small peek and see that Teddy is right. She is beautiful. Her long hair sways against her back and then flares out as she spins in circles. Her hands move as if they are outlining the movement of a calm wind.

Teddy wants to meet this woman and thinks that maybe, just maybe, she could teach me to dance like her. I remind Teddy that whoever comes through the door always leaves. No one ever wants to stay. I am tired of good-byes. Besides, who said I wanted to learn to dance? I hide my face.

The woman stays and continues to dance. Teddy tells me her body moves to the rhythm of her soft humming. He says her dress grabs the air as she spins. When she turns, her head and arms dip low and then swing up, swaying back and forth. She reminds him of an autumn maple tree with its branches moving in the wind. Helicopter leaves spin down to the ground.

I decide not to let Teddy look at her anymore. He should know better. I remind him that it's better not to get excited so that when she leaves, we won't miss her. She speaks and I listen, even though I do not move.

I've come to you little one. I thought I'd lost you, but I've finally found you. I've come to be your friend. I want to be someone you can trust. I will never leave you or ignore you. I know you can't believe these words now. I know it is hard to trust. But that's okay, because I will wait. You are terrified and think I could be dangerous, but one day you'll see that my love for you is safe.

My name is Me Ra. I am the woman who wouldn't let my little one inside wake up. I've been afraid of your pain and ignored your cries. Instead of helping you, I hushed you to sleep. You've been asleep for years. This dark room of my heart has been your hiding place. You tried to tell me you needed help. You tried to tell others you were scared and that bad things were happening. When no one believed you or even listened, you began to give up. You waited for so long, but no one came to the door. They were afraid of this room. I was afraid too. So you were left alone. And you rested your head on Teddy's lap and slept.

You've been asleep a long time now. The time has come to wake up. Your time of waiting is over. I am finally here to listen. I am here to open the door of this room so that it will never again be closed. Will you just glance at me, little one? Will you see the love on my face for you? It is still raining outside, and the dress I wear is black. But this time the falling rain is different and this dress will dance. This time I have heard your cry. You are the precious child in me. I have come to wake you up because the woman is incomplete without you. I need your innocence—the innocence only a child carries. The black of my dress will never let us forget your pain, but the rhythm of freedom is here to bring this dress to life. Can you hear it, my little one? Can you hear freedom beating in my every step?

During the months following the court procedures, I took care of myself as if I were a child. I needed to nurture this child. I couldn't ignore her pain ever again. However, the challenge was to find the balance between when to let myself feel the pain and when to put it on hold.

I was a full-time college student. I needed to both work and study, but the pain inside was only increasing. The man who raped me was allowed to re-enroll, since he was considered innocent until proven guilty. He followed me and asked others where I was. For seven months he stalked me. I would work at the information desk and he would sit at a table and just watch me. My telephone would ring at odd hours of the night. The caller hung up each time as soon as I said hello. I was always afraid but didn't have enough evidence to prove I was being stalked. While he worked hard at trying to control me, my fear grew and grew.

Some days I woke up crying. My counselor told me to talk to the child inside me when I was afraid. I would tell the little girl I had to go to class, but I would take time later to feel her pain. After classes, I would sometimes sit and color the way I did when I was five. It rested my mind and gave me a break from having to be this strong woman. Those times of coloring, and sometimes crying with my teddy bear, gave the Lord a chance to minister to the little girl inside of me. Those hours of resting in my Father's arms gave me strength to face each day and its demands.

After evening church services, my friend Alex would often take me out for coffee. We talked about how to handle my being harassed. On the outside, Alex would try to stay upbeat, encouraging and hopeful. But I knew that inside, even Alex felt like the situation was hopeless.

After seven months of being followed and indirectly harassed, I reached a breaking point. I didn't want to live anymore. I began to contemplate suicide. It was hard to see any hope for my future. People had always known me for my laughter, but now I rarely laughed about anything. The only way to survive was to find a way out of this place.

Being raped was like being hit by a truck no one could see. The collision was a nightmare that left me lying in the street, bleeding to death. There were no witnesses. No one called for help. I waited and waited to hear the siren of an ambulance. But no one came. No one could see that I was bleeding, because the bleeding was internal. I needed help; otherwise, I was going to die. I had lost the will to fight and I could feel the child in me once again being overwhelmed by fear.

I will never forget the Wednesday I walked into the chapel when Stephen Arterburn was the guest speaker. Tears began to run down my neck as we sang the worship songs. I knew my spirit was dying. I was glad when the speaker asked us to be seated, because my heart felt so heavy that I could hardly stand.

My attention drifted. Then Mr. Arterburn told us he wanted to talk about the reality of pain. My eyes fixed on him. I had never heard a speaker say the word "pain" as if there was no shame in acknowledging it. He said he knew that some of us were on the brink of depression. He said that even though we were attending a Christian university, he believed that some of us listening to him were also contemplating suicide. At that moment, I felt as if his eyes were looking at me. I wondered if he could see the hopelessness written on my face. I wanted to cover my head in shame, because I was one of those students.

He told us about New Life Clinics—the live-in clinics he had established as a safe place for hurting people to work through their pain. He said there was no shame in our getting help for ourselves. There was no shame in doing everything it took to choose life. He believed we were worthy of getting help.

When his speech was over, I wanted to go to him and tell him I was one of those people trying to run from depression. I wanted to ask him how I could get rid of all my suicidal thoughts. But I was afraid. If someone saw me talking to him, surely they would know I wasn't doing okay. We were all supposed to be Christians. I was the ministry leader on my floor. Christians have hope in Jesus, so they don't struggle with depression, right?

Maybe I wasn't the Christian I thought I was. Maybe I wasn't worthy to be at a school like this. Doubts began to cloud my mind. I walked out of the chapel and, at a distance, I could see the man who had raped me. He was talking with some other students. I had to pass them to get to my dorm. He looked up at me, said good-bye to his friends and just stood there. I looked down. When I walked by, I felt his eyes mock me. Seconds later, I heard someone laughing. I looked back and saw him—a couple hundred feet away and standing alone—laughing at me.

I picked up my pace and tried to act as if his laughter didn't bother me. Tears ran down my cheeks. When I got to my dorm, I collapsed in the bathroom. Was I really worthy of dropping all my responsibilities in the middle of the school quarter to get help? I thought of the chapel speaker saying there was no shame in taking care of yourself. Whether I felt worthy or not, if I didn't get help, I wasn't going to make it. I was bleeding to death, waiting for someone to see my pain and call the ambulance, yet no one was going to call the ambulance but me. So I spoke for myself. I called my mom and told her about the clinics.

The clinic was expensive. Our insurance wasn't going to cover the costs, and my mom and dad didn't know what to do. A counselor told my mom that I had had an emotional heart attack. I needed professional help if I was going to survive. That put the money issue into perspective for my parents. In the midst of their feeling helpless, they decided to take a risk.

Within three days, my dorm room was packed up and I withdrew from classes. Alex and my mom put me on a plane to Northern California, where I checked into the Christian clinic. I felt little hope that I would ever get better.

Part Two

Moving from Depression
to Grief

Is it true that Your tears roll down my face when I cry?

MY JOURNAL ENTRY

Chapter Three

Understanding Grief

~

Within that flame there may be torment, but there is no death.
Think well, my son, what dark ways we have trod. . . .
I guided you unharmed on Geryon: Shall I do no less
now we are nearer God?

DANTE, *DIVINE COMEDY*,
"PURGATORIO," CANTO XXVII

At the clinic, there was a sign identifying the psychiatric unit on the outside of double doors. I remember sitting and watching people walk past those doors. They would poke their faces into the window for a glimpse at a crazy person. *Does a crazy person look like me?* I wondered.

When I first got to the clinic, they took me into a room where a nurse searched my things. She took my hair dryer and perfume bottle. They didn't want to give me the chance to strangle myself with the hair-dryer cord or cut my wrists with the glass perfume bottle. I felt so ashamed. Was my pain this much of a threat to my well-being? Had I really come to this point?

A few months after the rape, I convinced everyone that I was just fine. Yes, I cried a lot. I slept 12 to 14 hours a day. I couldn't go anywhere without being afraid. I felt alone and ashamed of what had happened. But I was fine. Or I was going to be fine. I would tell people, "Don't worry about me. It's not that big of a deal anymore. It happened awhile ago."

I thought I was going through the healing process because I cried so much. Aren't tears supposed to be healing? They can be. But my tears were coming from the mire of depression. Depression isn't healing; only grief can heal. Both involve sadness; but grieving leads to hope, whereas depression leaves you hopeless.

I began to understand my condition when a friend gave me this description of the difference between depression and grieving. She said,

Depression is a bottomless pit. You can't see the top. You are too tired to even try to climb out. Grieving is being on top of the ground. It's like sitting on a park bench on a rainy day. Memories of the things you have lost pass by you. Every memory that passes by hurts and you feel the pain in the core of your being. Often you sit alone on the bench, but you are reachable. There is room for others to sit on the bench and remember with you. Tears flow because loss is always painful. Tears that honor what you have lost are shed, but they are not tears of hopelessness. They are tears that say good-bye and leave you free to move on.

Grief—the freeing kind—does not come naturally. To experience it requires you to face your feelings. I was afraid that if I started crying I might never stop. I felt that if I actually got angry about what had happened I might lose my mind and go crazy. I was afraid to feel the depth of the hurt and anger I held inside.

The process of grieving is such a long journey. It allows no shortcuts. Yet in the end, it always brings freedom. Before the end, there are mountains to climb. I didn't know the first thing about being a mountain climber. But at the clinic I met people who did.

The whole first week at the clinic went by quickly. I sat in the hall staring at the floor, my eyes a witness to the fact that my spirit was vacant of hope. On the outside, I looked emotionless; on the inside, I was screaming with rage that demanded to know why I was the one locked in the psychiatric ward instead of the man who had raped me. My rage focused on wanting to have my life, my virginity, my innocence, my hope and my joy back.

I had been raised to believe that anger was not acceptable and, if exercised, always ended up hurting someone else. My rage had no place to go. Instead of coming out, it brewed inside of me.

Until the day Mark approached me, I did nothing but let time go by. Mark was a fellow patient who was getting ready to go home within a week. He must have been in his late 40s or early 50s, like most of the other patients. I will never forget his face. It glowed with a certain peace.

Mark walked up to me and introduced himself. He took one look at me and said, "Me Ra, you'll get out of this as much as you put into it. The longer you sit there and deny any of your pain, the longer it will rule your life.

"Look around you. All the other patients are twice your age. Why do you think that is? It's because we did what you're doing right now for most of our lives. We ignored our pain and just stuffed it down. But one day it all exploded, and that's why we're here. Except we're not 19; we're parents, grandparents, wives, husbands . . . and our grief has multiplied itself. Do you see how much you have to gain if you will invest yourself in your time at this clinic?"

And that was it. He said what he had to say and left me by myself in the hallway where he had found me. I felt myself crumble. He was challenging me to be more than a victim; he was challenging me to be a conqueror. I was scared to death to move.

His words burned into me. In fact, they haunted me that night. I lay awake in bed and let the pain begin to surface. Tears finally came for the first time in a week. Then, eventually, sleep came. The next morning I attended my first group-therapy session. I had been going to them all week, but for the first time, I was emotionally present and ready to deal with the pain inside of me.

For the next few weeks I went through eight to twelve hours of therapy a day—sometimes individual sessions and sometimes group sessions. One of the times, when it was my turn in group, the therapist re-created the night I was raped, using the furniture in the room. I was reluctant to do the exercise, not understanding how an empty chair next to me was supposed to feel like the car seat I had sat on on that Valentine's Day night. When the therapist said "Go" to the group and the group helped reenact the scene, I held on to my therapist's hand to get me through the scariest night of my life—for a second time. In that intimate therapy session, I was given the chance to stop the rape and step out of the car. I crawled out of the chair feeling all the shame and helplessness I had felt before.

When it was over, all nine other patients stood on one side of the room and, with guidance from the therapist, said in unison, "We are stepping in in place of the woman judge who hurt you.

We are a jury to replace the judge you had in court. We believe you, Me Ra. We believe you were raped. And we hear your voice. We hear you."

There had been no jury for the simple restraining order court procedure, but the power of my group's words that day brought deep validation to my spirit. Tears of grief released themselves. I cried and I cried. And it was finally healing to cry.

At the clinic, I found myself in a place made up of mountain climbers. Those patients became my family over the next month. I have never seen pain like I saw there. And I have never laughed as hard as I did there. I learned that as deep as our pain might be, God's joy can always go deeper.

Together we climbed our mountains of pain. Together we cried.

Sometimes we weren't allowed to hug the person who was crying. We couldn't even touch them. The clinic was teaching us a different kind of comfort. It was a comfort that let people cry until the tears stopped. How many times have I hushed or patted away someone's pain, telling them it was okay, because I was afraid to see the reality of their hurt? How much more powerful it is to sit with a person and accept the reality of the pain, realizing that the tears are necessary, every last one!

Releasing my anger was another mountain I knew I had to climb before leaving the clinic. I remember feeling my anger begin to rumble. I was continuously agitated and restless. I was scared. I had climbed the mountain of grief, but the mountain of anger loomed 10 times higher. I thought Christians weren't supposed to ever be in a rage—or even angry, for that matter. And I had plenty of rage inside.

We could all see the time coming for me to face this issue. Before the next group session, I asked Michael, the Jamaican nurse, to promise me he would put me in a straitjacket if I got so angry in group that I went ballistic. I had to know that someone would be in control and able to help me. I was convinced that my anger would drive me to lose all sanity. Michael reminded me that safety was why I had come to the clinic. But that didn't make me feel better. Did Michael think I'd go crazy?

During the session, the therapist again keyed in on me. But instead of getting angry, I started to cry. I'll never forget when the therapist got right in my face and said in a strong voice, "Me Ra, this isn't the time to cry. Crying is different from being angry. You know you're hurt, but now is the time to be mad about the fact that you were robbed. Stop crying and let out your anger!"

I didn't know how. I'd never really been angry in a healthy way. It took many more sessions before the anger and rage finally released itself. And you know what? Michael never needed to get a straitjacket for me.

At the clinic, I did the hardest thing I will ever do. I chose to stop running and to look my pain straight in the face. I saw all of its rawness and, for the first time, I didn't turn away. I looked at it for what it was and embraced it, instead of acting as if it didn't exist.

Some people shift in their seats when I tell them I was once a patient at a clinic. Other people admire my survival. But survival isn't the goal; overcoming is. One of the first lessons I learned at the clinic was that I wasn't part of a group of odd people; we weren't "crazy," unable to cope with life. We were people who had chosen to try to be honest with our pain. And this made us human. This made us real. We were people choosing to be overcomers.

Was I all better at the end of the month? No. I felt like I'd only begun the healing process. A month before, I had walked in through those double doors with no hope. Now I was getting ready to walk out with mountain-climbing tools for the journey still ahead. I had come through so much healing in a month, yet life still didn't feel fully worth living. Would I make it? Only time would tell.

Even though I was scared to leave the clinic, it would be wonderful to see familiar faces again. I left a message with Alex, letting him know when I'd be home, because he had promised to meet me at the airport.

Chapter Four

The Suicide

~

Wait without thought, for you are not ready for thought: so the darkness shall be the light, and the stillness the dancing.

T. S. ELIOT, *FOUR QUARTETS*,
"EAST COKER," III

In three days I would be released from the clinic. Many of the patients who had been in the clinic when I arrived were now gone. They had all successfully graduated and gone back to their families.

I was still attending my group and individual therapy sessions, but it wasn't the same. The tools they were teaching us were no longer new and difficult to understand; they had become a part of my life. I found myself encouraging the new patients to work for their healing, just as Mark had encouraged me.

When a voice through the intercom asked me to report to the nurses' station, I secretly wondered if they were going to surprise me with a going-away present. I walked down the hallway and saw my individual counselor standing at the station. He only came to the clinic for our appointments and I knew we didn't have an appointment scheduled for that day. I waved and smiled at him, but he didn't smile or wave back.

"Me Ra," he said, "we need to talk in private." His voice was steady and serious.

I glanced at the two nurses in the station. They were struggling to smile at me.

When we were in a private room and sitting down, my counselor said, "Me Ra, your friend Alex committed suicide."

My whole body froze. I looked at his eyes as he repeated the words, but I couldn't hear his voice. Everything went silent around me. All I remember is grabbing my heart. The pain of what I was hearing made my heart physically ache. I wondered if I was having a heart attack. My body became weak and I felt myself fall to the floor in a faint. Everything seemed to be in slow motion. One of the nurses came running in and gave me a shot, but I don't remember much else from the rest of that day or night.

Fortunately, my release date from the clinic did not change. They understood that I wanted to be at Alex's funeral. Part of me could not believe he had died; it was all just a misunderstanding that I needed to figure out.

I wrote the following allegory as I tried to process the rape and Alex's death. Together, they were the demon who rushed through the house of my heart, destroying everything. I pleaded for the demon to stop, but he didn't. When it was over, my heart was like a house of ruins. Even as I wrote out of my hurt, I could not ignore a tiny light in my house of darkness. It was a light I had found in the clinic—a divine presence that surrounded me. God knew that I needed it most right now. I called her Stillness, my messenger from God.

She loved me the way I needed to be loved, even though it took a long time for me to realize her love was what I needed. I had always thought loving someone meant that you took away their pain. If you truly loved them, you would take away all their fears and calm all their doubts. Right?

Stillness did none of these things. She loved me with a greater love. Her love was often silent. She knew there were no words that could comfort the depths of my hurt. She knew that to hush away my tears would only cause more pain, yet her form crouched in agony at seeing me in pain. Love that allows for mourning brings healing.

As much as I wanted someone to erase the rape and suicide from my life, I realized that I had a bigger need. Once again, I wanted someone to feel my hurt, to cry for me when I couldn't cry, to be angry for me when I had no will to care, to believe for me when I had forgotten there was a word called "hope." That's when Stillness came.

Death. How unfair you are. You creep up to the house of my heart. You don't knock at my front door; instead you come like a tornado through the back door and invade my house—my heart.

Filled with rage, you run through the rooms and turn off all the lights. You throw everything outside. I am left feeling helpless, exposed, out of control. Now you occupy my house. I bang on the doors and windows. I pull my hair and watch the anxiety in me turn my knuckles white. I yell and scream, "Leave this place! Oh, please, please leave me!" There is no answer. You are gone. Your plan was never to stay—only to destroy.

You leave my heart in ruins. The memories call out to me from every direction. I walk back into the house, picking up memories.

I am consumed with loss. I am becoming loss. The loss of laughter, peace and worth all taunt me. I can hear past memories call my name. They are so alive, yet their substance is nowhere to be found. I feel hot tears on my face. I am wordless, thoughtless. I am dying. I am becoming a being of death.

Then comes the emptiness. It penetrates my soul. I am slowly fading and cannot control what is happening. I claw at the walls and scream out to God, "Let me out of this prison of a house. Don't leave me alone with the remains of death. I will not survive. The pain is too great." God's voice answers in silence.

Darkness captures me. All that was important does not matter anymore. Life is nowhere to be found. I have no other option but to simply sit. I am not waiting. To wait is to hope, and I have nothing to hope for.

Grotesque creatures wearing masks with deceiving smiles ask if they can move in. They want to eliminate the vacancy the many deaths have left. They say they know the loneliness in my heart and they understand how deep it pierces. They try to convince me they can rid me of the emptiness. But when death came, it stole everything. I have nothing to give, no trust to offer—not even to them. Why are they so eager? I watch my vulnerability and pain inflame their joy.

I don't feel that I can trust God; but my fear of these taunting creatures who are urging me to end the pain overwhelms me, and I am too weak to tell them to go. I cry out to God in my helplessness. As fast as my heart cries out and unspoken words release themselves in desperate pleas, there is silence. The tempters have vanished. Their bargaining is over. The pain in my heart throbs. The deceiving voices are gone, but the hole is only deeper. It is quiet now. Silence awaits me.

Days go by, weeks and now months—over half a year has passed—and I am still sitting here. Stillness is the only one present. She seems to care for me. But if so, why doesn't she take the pain away or fill the void left by the many deaths? She quietly sits with me and waits. Her quietness grates on my heart's impatience. Why doesn't she do something? At times I get upset with her and challenge her. "If you really care, you would take this all away." She doesn't reply. She only listens. Yet over time her waiting becomes healing. I begin to realize that even though this healing is painful, it is real. I am thankful for her presence.

One day, she gets up and fear overwhelms me. "Don't leave!" my heart cries. "Don't leave now! I need you here." I watch in dread as she walks to one side of the house. Instead of leaving, she reaches for the curtains. I cower, bending my head toward my lap, anticipating a light too bright to bear. The darkness of this house has become everything. Darkness is my home. Stillness pulls the curtains open to help me see beyond the darkness.

No bright light attacks me. Instead, I open my eyes to find it is night outside. I walk to the window and see the world of stars above me. I had long forgotten those precious dots of light, shining out of a black sea. They work solely to keep the darkness from consuming the night. They do not deny the fact that it is dark; they bring bits of light into the dark.

From the corner of my eye I see Stillness moving. As her eyes search the dark heavens, she slowly begins to transform. My eyes squinch in disbelief at what I am seeing. She herself is light.

She is a glimpse of heaven sent by God to sit in all my nights. She did not come to take my night away but to be with me so that darkness could never consume me. No matter how deep my loneliness, she was never shaken by my fear. She sat beside me through the numbness and every painful feeling. As I began to accept her presence and help, I began to desire life.

I pleaded for death and You, O God, answered by bringing me Your servant, Stillness. Her light has become a piece of new life in me.

Sadness was a big part of my grieving. Do you find yourself trying to put words to your sadness, yet failing? Do you feel as if death has invaded your life?

Maybe you go through your day and for a few hours you feel really good; but by evening you feel down again. Dearest sister, you are not crazy. You are not going insane. You are not manic-depressive. You are probably grieving. Sadness is the cloud that rests on your heart until the grieving is done and there are no more tears of loss to cry.

When a woman is raped, many things are taken from her: assurance in herself, trust in men, a sense of safety. Sometimes you don't know these things are gone until you realize you can't trust. I grieved the loss of each one of these things before they were ever restored. Grieving is a process; it takes time. Being called to wait goes against our nature. But time does heal.

Right now, are you living in the night? When you look out the windows of your soul, hoping to see the bright sun, are you disappointed by the darkness? If so, will you look up to the sky with me? Will you squint your eyes with whatever hope you have left? Will you strain to see the stars? They are so small, yet they are tiny bits of light in your nights of grief. Let the emptiness of your night bring Stillness to your heart as we wait together for the rising sun.

Chapter Five

Sisters

~

The eye cannot say to the hand, "I don't need you!" And the head cannot say to the feet, "I don't need you!" On the contrary, those parts of the body that seem to be weaker are indispensable, and the parts that we think are less honorable we treat with special honor. And the parts that are unpresentable are treated with special modesty, while our presentable parts need no special treatment. But God has combined the members of the body and has given greater honor to the parts that lacked it, so that there should be no division in the body, but that its parts should have equal concern for each other. If one part suffers, every part suffers with it; if one part is honored, every part rejoices with it. Now you are the body of Christ, and each one of you is a part of it.

1 CORINTHIANS 12:21-27

I once read these words on a greeting card: "I walked a mile with sorrow and never a word said she; but, oh, the things I learned from her when sorrow walked with me." Jesus didn't give me Joy as a companion to walk me out of the clinic doors; He gave me deep sadness. The cloud of sadness lingered over my head as I waited for the taxi to come pick me up and take me to the airport. I decided to call that sadness Sorrow. I think Sorrow is a sister to Grief and Stillness. Sorrow doesn't say much; she just keeps you company. She held my hand and we waited for the taxi together.

When the plane landed but before it came to a complete stop, passengers were clicking open their seat belts and jumping into the aisles. I was probably the only one who wasn't in a hurry to get off. I looked out the window, then at the back of the chair in front of me and then at the people in a stand-still line. Every passenger had somewhere to go. For everyone except me, life would continue to move ahead and no one would object. The stand-still line moved too quickly.

Whether I felt ready or not, my life was beginning a new chapter. Even though Alex had committed suicide, the option of suicide for me was leaving my mind. I felt weak and vulnerable from just being released from a clinic, but I wanted to try school again. Fall quarter would start in less than two months.

The clinic had advised me to make a schedule for myself. They suggested getting a part-time job before school started. It was important to have something to focus on other than the pain and my healing process. So I found a job and looked for a place to live.

When my girlfriends from college heard I was coming back to school, they asked me to live with them. It was an answer to prayer, but it also scared me. They weren't like the people I'd been with in the clinic for the last month. And they certainly weren't trained counselors. They were at ease with their femininity, but I was still struggling with the myth that my femininity had been the cause of the rape. They were comfortable wearing dresses and skirts. I only wore dark colors and baggy clothes that hid my figure.

We were four women in a one-and-a-half bathroom apartment and had to sign up for bathroom time slots. We slowly became a body within ourselves. Each woman had her own gifts, strengths and weaknesses. Each of us had something unique to share. But I was like the eye who said to the hand, "I don't need you!"

When I first began living with my new roommates, I thought they were "weaker" than I. Unless you had been raped, had suffered the death of a loved one, had been abused or spent time in a clinic, you couldn't relate to me. Pride twisted my brokenness into a subtle arrogance and self-centeredness. In my insecurity, I let my pain give me permission to feel better than others. My friends had taken me into their apartment, hoping to be a support to me; I, in return, mocked their attempts to try to help something they didn't understand. In reality, the truly weak member of this small living body of believers was me.

One roommate, Lynne, frustrated me greatly during our first six months together. Structure and consistency were two of her many gifts. Lynne would get up every morning to read her Bible and pray. Then she would copy a special verse for me and leave it on my pillow, telling me she'd be praying for me throughout the day. Each Scripture always seemed to have the same message: God loved me and had a plan for my life. At the time, I was repulsed by her attempts to comfort me. What did she understand about my life? Nonetheless, in the midst of my unpredictable and unstable emotions, Lynne's consistency gave me comfort. If everything felt like it was falling apart around me, I always knew Lynne would be praying for me the next morning and every morning to follow.

My part-time job was at a small catering company. When I wasn't at home with my three roommates, I was at work with three women, cooking. The job helped me to slowly enter the outside world from which the clinic had hidden me for a time. I would cook for four hours, three times a week. It was therapeutic and also gave me a break from "feeling" my emotions so much. But whenever I came back home to the safety of our apartment, tears still surfaced easily.

No matter what had happened to them during the day, if my roommates came home and saw me crying, they would sit beside me. They never pretended to have the answers; they just wanted to be there, so I wouldn't have to cry alone. And in the midst of their care, I remained frozen . . . proud . . . but, most of all, scared and alone.

You see, Satan didn't want me to get better. He doesn't want any of us to get better, let alone get free. He hates unity, love and healing. He hates me and he hates you; yet you listen to him and so do I, because inside our hearts, God doesn't make sense. We're angry at the injustice of this society. We despise the fact that the innocent are victimized. And we cry out to God, "Where are You, omnipotent God?" And we hear silence.

In the silence of Love that is ever present but not always understandable in our pain, the deceiver and manipulator of truth speaks up. He would challenge me by the minute. He would say in my thoughts, "Tell me, if God really cares, why didn't He do something? After all, God had the power to enter that car and stop the rape. What is love but to protect the ones you love from being hurt? And what about your roommates? They don't care. How can they if they don't really understand your situation? Me Ra, listen to reason. You got better at the clinic. Don't throw it all away by thinking you can trust another person's love for you."

We make a mistake when we forget how clever the devil is. More than a source of general evil, he knows exactly what our needs are and how to twist truth to bring us to the point of dis-trusting God and separating ourselves from help.

The truth is, no person understands. It's a truth I must remind myself of daily. Only God knows the details of my heart. I could search the corners of the earth and find countless men and women who have been raped, yet none would ever know exactly how I feel. That doesn't mean no one can help. God uses many different people to usher in His healing.

The enemy of our souls also knows how to compound con-fusion. Many times in those early days of grief, I would replay the rape over and over. I thought that if I could just find the moment I had "asked for it," I could ask God to forgive me and it would all go away. At the same time, I knew I had not invited the violation and didn't know how I could have done anything more to prevent myself from being overpowered. I was so con-fused. All I had were three voices: mine, Satan's and God's. For some reason, it was so hard to hear God's voice and mine. God knew I needed my roommates. He intended them to be part of His voice to me.

If you can relate to the feelings I had about believing that my roommates couldn't help me unless they had lived in my darkness, I must tell you something else. Don't let Satan steal more than he already has. Pain isolates us from people. We cannot escape this fact. But pain does not have to shut people out of our lives.

Satan wants us to live in isolation. He wants us to believe that no one else can help us. He is a thief who wants to rob us of all our hope and joy. He doesn't want life for us. He wants us to walk through our days feeling condemned, ashamed and guilty. He wants memories of the rape to run an endless loop through our minds as we try to find something we could have done to prevent it.

You and I were both victims when we said no and the people we thought we could trust didn't listen, but instead they forced themselves on us. You are innocent. I am innocent. Don't let Satan keep you wrestling with a lie or keep you locked into false pride that tells you no one else can understand, no one else can help. When we develop friendships with people whom we can love and trust, we catch a glimpse of God.

It is a great comfort to know that God loves us and is with us all the time, no matter what else happens; He Himself will be our friend. But the truth is, Jesus longs to love us through each other too. He wants to speak to you through the voices of others who know and love Him. He longs to hold you through their arms. He desires to laugh with you through their joy. He celebrates our smallest victories through their belief in us. And He renews our hearts through their love.

Ask God for a support system and caring friends. Consider joining a support group. Don't be discouraged if it takes a while, and don't forget that pain often makes us feel alone even when surrounded by caring people. I believe that God will answer your heart's cry for the support you need.

Chapter Six

Breaking Plates

———

You are not limited by your past. You are only limited by the weights you refuse to release.

T. D. JAKES, *DADDY LOVES HIS GIRLS*

I had begun to learn about anger while I was in the clinic. But I still had a long way to go in knowing how to recognize it, express it safely and use it to teach me about myself.

One Sunday afternoon, I came home from church feeling hurt and frustrated. Someone had approached me during the service and within minutes pushed every red button I had. Do you ever have those encounters? It's as if some people know exactly how to make you mad, and they enjoy doing it. At the apartment, I walked straight through the doorway and stomped up the stairs. I intentionally ignored Taylor and Emma's greetings, which was code for "Follow me upstairs and ask me what's the matter."

Even before they walked through the bedroom door, I was rambling about my frustration. My voice sounded harsh and loud. I wanted to yell to let the anger out, but I couldn't. I cried off and on while pacing back and forth, but I couldn't find words to express the turmoil inside. Emma and Taylor didn't know what to think.

Then something switched inside me. What I couldn't express, I hid from. I quit rambling and just stared as the tears silently began to multiply.

Emma grabbed my arm and said, "Come on, Me Ra. You are not stuffing this anger; it's coming out today if it's the last thing we do!" Taylor grabbed my jacket and they led me downstairs.

Emma and Taylor understood the feeling of wanting to hurt the person who hurts you. However, retaliation isn't constructive or even realistic. But the hurt still pushes for expression. So we turn it against ourselves or end up hurting an innocent friend or family member. Instead of getting our anger out in a constructive way, we multiply the hurt by allowing it to fester inside or by saying destructive things to someone. Either way, someone gets hurt again.

I hadn't known there were healthy ways to express anger until the clinic taught me; it also taught me that breaking plates worked the best. My roommates and I had been saving a bag of old porcelain plates under the sink for just this moment.

With me placed securely in the middle, the three of us walked arm in arm to a quiet side street with no houses or cars. Taylor handed me the first plate. I took it and just stood there. The idea of breaking plates sounded stupid. I felt like such a hypocrite. Here I'd been telling the girls how important it is to release your anger, and I'd forgotten how hard it can be. So Emma took the plate and came to my rescue.

She held it in her hands and talked about how perfect and beautiful it was. Then with a loud yell that made both Taylor and me jump, she threw the plate. With a sigh of relief she turned and looked at us and said, "Ooooh, that felt good. Your turn, Me Ra." Taylor and I looked at each other and started giggling.

Without even trying, Emma designed a three-step process to break plates. First, you must look at the plate and comment on its beauty and perfection. Second, you wind back with your throwing arm and yell out something you're frustrated about. Third, you throw the plate with all your might and watch it shatter.

I decided to try it. But when I took a plate, my mind went blank. Can you believe it? I couldn't think of anything to yell. Emma kindly refreshed my memory about the hurtful encounter at church. I finally wound back my arm and yelled out one of my many hurts. We watched the plate shatter. It was freeing, and it worked. I threw another plate and another. Then tears began to stream down my face. I stopped. Letting my anger out was like releasing another layer of grief that was deeper than the church conversation. Everything in me wanted to sit down and cry.

"Me Ra," Emma said, "I know you want to cry, but right now it's not time to be sad. I want you to be angry."

Taylor handed me another plate, and I kept going until my anger felt fully released. When it was over, I was thoroughly exhausted. But I felt alive.

As I watched the girls pick up the broken pieces, I saw my heart in those shattered plates. People I had trusted and loved had taken my heart and, like a porcelain plate, thrown it down and then walked away.

As the girls searched for the small slivers as well as the big pieces, I heard Jesus speak to my heart. "Me Ra," He said, "these are the pieces of your heart. I am going to find every single broken piece and make for you a new heart, a heart after Me."

He's doing the same for you.

Chapter Seven

Sleepless Nights

—~—

I woke up crying last night. Why? I'm not really sure. I don't cry as much as I used to. In fact, things have been better in the last two months or so. As Taylor would graciously say, "I've been living victoriously." Last night I felt defeated.

JOURNAL ENTRY TWO YEARS AFTER THE RAPE

I have yet to meet a rape victim who has not fallen victim to sleep disturbance. Before the rape, I loved bedtime. I relished the feel of tucking myself into bed with lots of blankets and leaving the window open wide. The room would be freezing, but I was warm because I was bundled in bed. While growing up, I remember priding myself on being able to sleep through anything.

That all changed after the rape. Sleep became an enemy. For two years, sleep for me was like entering a stretch of dark heaviness.

Almost every night the man who had raped me invaded my dreams. Either I was attacking him or running from him in fear of being raped again. Often I would wake up crying hysterically, my sweaty pajamas sticking to my body. I was afraid to go to sleep. I feared I wouldn't wake up when the nightmares came and would somehow be trapped all over again. At the same time, the anger coming out in my dreams frightened me.

My roommates prayed with and for me that I would sleep free of nightmares, but the nightmares still came. Who would wake me when I was trapped in the swirling darkness of a dream? Every night I would ask myself the question: *Where is God in the night?* His lack of protection in my dreams upset me.

Night after night, my three roommates, not knowing how to help, helped anyway. They sat beside my bed and took turns singing, reading Bible verses and stroking my brow until I fell asleep.

Lynne and Emma slept in a room down the hall, but Taylor slept in the bunk right above me. I remember feeling insecure about who would have to share a room with me when I got out of the clinic. Taylor took care of that concern before I had a chance to verbalize it. She would have it no other way but to be my roommate.

She remembers my asking her the same question night after night: "Taylor, do you think you could wake me up if you hear me having a nightmare?"

She always answered, "Of course, Me Ra."

No matter when the nightmares came, her precious voice would lead me out. "Me Ra," she would say, "you're okay. You're in the apartment with me, Taylor. You're safe, Me Ra."

Taylor is a heavy sleeper, so it never ceased to amaze me that God would wake her up when I desperately needed someone to be awake with me. An alarm clock blaring at full volume for 30 minutes beside Taylor's head could not wake her up for class. Yet small nudges by God's Spirit never failed.

Being able to sleep was another mountain to climb, and it was much higher than I had expected. To climb it successfully, I had to understand it. I learned through counseling that those terrifying dreams stemmed from my anger with the rape. The more I released my anger, the less frequently the nightmares would come. As time went on, I stopped attacking the man in my dreams and he stopped chasing me. Finally, a time of rest came.

I thought God had left me that year. But all along He had been sitting at my bedside, singing songs to me, reading me His Word, brushing my brow and speaking His comfort in the middle of the night.

During the most intense times of troubled sleep, I wondered if night would ever again be a time of restorative rest. It would have seemed absurd to even think of night in terms of restoration.

I know that many of you also feel as if the mountain of peaceful sleep looms high. Some of you will climb that mountain tonight; others of you are standing at the base of the mountain, feeling defeated. May I give you the mountain-climbing tools my roommates and I used—tools I still use today? These are some of the key verses the girls would pray with me. When no one had the right words to say, we were always amazed at how peace would fill the room when we started reading God's Word aloud. I pray that as you or someone close to you reads these verses out loud during your sleepless nights, you will experience peace, strength and, most of all, restful sleep.

Me Ra's Mountain-Climbing Tools

On my bed I remember you; I think of you through the watches of the night. Because you are my help, I sing in the shadow of your wings (Ps. 63:6,7).

I cried out to God for help; I cried out to God to hear me. When I was in distress, I sought the Lord; at night I stretched out untiring hands and my soul refused to be comforted (Ps. 77:1,2).

When I awake, I am still with you (Ps. 139:18, my favorite).

At midnight I rise to give you thanks for your righteous laws. My eyes stay open through the watches of the night, that I may meditate on your promises. Those who devise wicked schemes are near, but they are far from your law. Yet you are near, O LORD, and all your commands are true. Look upon my suffering and deliver me (Ps. 119:62,148,150,151,153).

I lie awake; I have become like a bird alone on a roof (Ps. 102:7).

Though you probe my heart and examine me at night,
though you test me, you will find nothing; I have
resolved that my mouth will not sin (Ps. 17:3).

I will praise the LORD, who counsels me; even at night
my heart instructs me (Ps. 16:7).

I am worn out from groaning; all night long I flood
my bed with weeping and drench my couch with tears.
My eyes grow weak with sorrow; they fail because
of all my foes (Ps. 6:6,7).

For His anger lasts only a moment, but his favor lasts
a lifetime; weeping may remain for a night, but
rejoicing comes in the morning (Ps. 30:5).

I will refresh the weary and satisfy the faint (Jer. 31:25).

The LORD your God is with you, He is mighty
to save. He will take great delight in you, he will quiet
you with his love, he will rejoice over you
with singing (Zeph. 3:17).

Be still [precious child], and know that I am God
(Ps. 46:10).

Who is this coming up from the desert like a column of
smoke, perfumed with myrrh and incense made from
all the spices of the merchant? Look! It is Solomon's
carriage, escorted by sixty warriors, the noblest of Israel,
all of them wearing the sword, all experienced in battle,

each with his sword at his side, prepared for the terrors of the night (Song of Songs 3:6-8).

I took you from the ends of the earth, from its farthest corners I called you. I said, "You are my servant"; I have chosen you and have not rejected you (Isa. 41:9).

Do you not know? Have you not heard? The LORD is the everlasting God, the Creator of the ends of the earth. He will not grow tired or weary, and his understanding no one can fathom (Isa. 40:28).

Isaiah 43 (the whole chapter)

I will lead the blind by ways they have not known, along unfamiliar paths I will guide them; I will turn the darkness into light before them and make the rough places smooth. These are the things I will do; I will not forsake them (Isa. 42:16).

My people will live in peaceful dwelling places, in secure homes, in undisturbed places of rest (Isa. 32:18).

O LORD, be gracious to us; we long for you. Be our strength every morning, our salvation in time of distress (Isa. 33:2).

For your Maker is your husband—the LORD Almighty is his name (Isa. 54:5).

"I have seen his ways, but I will heal him; I will guide him and restore comfort to him, creating praise on the lips of the mourners in Israel. Peace, peace, to those far and near," says the LORD. "And I will heal them" (Isa. 57:18,19).

Then you will call, and the LORD will answer; you will cry for help, and he will say: Here am I (Isa. 58:9).

Part Three

Stepping into the Light

Does the light of Your dawn reach every hidden corner?

MY JOURNAL ENTRY

Chapter Eight

The 18 Lies You Don't Need to Own

Everything that deceives may be said to enchant.

PLATO

Graduation was coming. Lynne, Emma, Taylor and I would all be moving on. I knew this meant that I would have to fight the internal battles I still sometimes faced without the help of Taylor sleeping above me or Emma and Lynne down the hall. But I knew this would be okay.

My church had become a significant support network for me, and there were also older people—mentors—who checked in on me regularly. The Lord brings us many different support groups throughout our healing journey. It is hard to believe we will grow out of needing so much from people, yet we do, and it's good to know we will become stronger.

What we believe about ourselves during the process of healing is of the utmost importance, because we can either tell ourselves the truth or we can tell ourselves lies.

I had many lies in my head that I needed to get rid of. I once asked my counselor how to go about doing that. She gently smiled at me and told me what she pictured lies to be. She said they were like bad tapes playing over and over in our thoughts. The only way to get rid of them was to insert a truth tape in our minds. Although the lies wouldn't just disappear, the truth tapes would eventually become so loud and so familiar that the lies would sound like faint whispers in the far distance.

Sometimes the devil whispers in our ears and we can instantly identify his words as lies. At other times the lies are not so obvious. Sometimes our support system of people can help us fight off the lies. At other times, we need to fight on our own.

Before graduation, I sat down with my mom and wrote out the top 18 lies that played in my head. Everyone around me could tell me they were lies, but I needed to believe that for myself. I wanted these lies out of my mind, overshadowed by the tapes of truth.

Maybe some of these lies sound familiar to you. I can finally see the falsehood in each one, but there was a time when I couldn't. Read over the lies and laugh with me if you can, or add your comments to mine.

Me Ra's 18 Lies

1. I am hopeless.
2. I could have tried harder, so why didn't I?
3. I am not beautiful; I am ugly.
4. I'm not good enough; I am dirty and impure.

5. God can't use me!
6. If people knew the real me, they would reject me.
7. When people see me with men, they're thinking that I'm a slut.
8. I'm never going to get married.
9. I'm never going to have a family, especially a healthy one.
10. I can't encourage anyone.
11. I'm a failure at life!
12. I can't be normal. I hate my life.
13. Since I've been raped once, I will be raped again.
14. Nobody cares and nobody wants to understand. They are too involved in their own problems.
15. My friends are tired of hearing me cry about the same things.
16. There is no way a man could ever care about me. Just look at me. Who would want to be with me?
17. I'm not going to make it through this.
18. I will always be a victim.

What do you think of this list of lies?

Look at the lie that reads "I can't encourage anyone." Does that mean never?

What about number 12: "I can't be normal"? I still wonder what it means to be normal and if I really want that.

Try number 2. Maybe, like me, you keep hearing in your head the voice that says you could have done something to prevent the rape. This is Satan's favorite lie to throw at me when I'm down.

Satan's second favorite lie with me has been number 16, combined with 8 and 9. He has tried to tell me I would never get married, or if I did, I would not be worthy of marrying a healthy person. Why? Because if the man I married wasn't healthy, then at least he would understand and maybe accept me. This lie makes us feel like our experience disqualifies us from intimate relationships with healthy people.

Another lie I particularly want to bring to light is number 15: "My friends are tired of hearing me cry about the same things." If you think your friends are tired of listening to you, help your friends to help you. Let them know where it hurts—again. Pediatricians say that one of the most frustrating parts of their job is to watch a baby cry. The baby has no words to express where it hurts. But we have the words.

The second and implied part of that lie is "I'm not getting better, because I'm still crying about the same things." Lie. Lie. Lie. It's okay if you're crying about the same things three years later. I was. I may still cry about it even 20 years from now. But I'm getting better, and so will you.

The last lie, number 18, says "I will always be a victim." This lie is probably the most deceiving one of all, because we sometimes think we want to be a victim. We think there is safety in being a victim. Without fully realizing it at the time, I believed—I hoped—that if I stayed helpless and needy, I wouldn't be hurt again. I would always have my mom or my girlfriends looking after me, and people would be more sensitive toward me. I didn't realize that around my neck I was wearing an invisible sign: "Take advantage of me. I believe I'm always going to be a helpless victim." We would be surprised to see how many predators have the secret decoder glasses to read those signs we wear.

Lie 18 is the echo behind every other lie above it. If you and I choose to believe the truth—that we are not victims and that God is in our lives and does have healing and wholeness for us—

then we have to refuse all 18 lies, which say in one way or another that our identities are tied to being victims.

Holding on to a victim identity does not keep us safe from further harm, either externally or internally. In fact, if we do not choose to take off the victim sign from our necks, the reverse is true. The outcome can be dangerous. I hear the stories of men and women who were molested as children, raped as teenagers and now are married to abusive spouses. Of course, the issues of abuse involve more than a refusal to play the victim; but healing does involve release of the victim role.

The more we choose not to wear the sign of the victim, the less we are plagued by the effects of its invisible presence. Walking through this life with a sensitive heart is work, because opening your heart to love gives someone the potential to hurt you. In fact, risking to love and trust again is impossible without God.

To live fully, the lies must go. I don't believe, however, that from one day to the next we can decide once and for all not to believe our lies and to refuse the role of a victim. I wish I could tell you that if you go through enough counseling and work on your issues and you get prayer and support from a network of friends and your church, then you'll be totally free of the pain in your past—totally free from your monsters. I have done all these things and the pain still lingers. Some days I must choose over and over again not to have the mind-set of a victim, although the need to do so lessens as time goes on. The tapes of truth are becoming louder and louder.

When I think about the power the lies exercised over my life, I know it is God's grace that allows me to hear the truth. This is freedom. It is like the child who wakes up after a tormenting night to find that what she thought was a monster in her closet is only a shadow. These 18 lies were my shadows, trying to convince me that a monster lived inside me.

The day my mom sat with me and wrote down the 18 lies, they were all I knew to believe. How beautiful it was for her to take me seriously, knowing that at that time, those 18 lies were my reality. Although the pain they sprang from was real, they were not the whole story.

Lies are purely lies, and the truth will always be the truth. If you don't have strength to fight your own version of these 18 lies and take off the victim sign from around your neck, then write down all your lies like I did. Hide that piece of paper away. What a glorious day it will be when you stumble across your list of lies and find yourself no longer feeling like a victim and able to smile at how far you've come.

Chapter Nine

Climbing Up to the Garden

—◁▷—

*From the depths of the earth you will again bring me up. You will
increase my honor and comfort me once again.*

PSALM 71:20,21

After graduation, I was looking for a new place to live. Lynne was
getting married, Taylor was soon to be engaged, and Emma was
on her way to England. The Lord led me to an older couple's
house. Their own children were married and gone, and they were
more than willing to have a young person in their home again.

I still found myself walking in the shadows cast by the rape
and Alex's suicide, but I felt much stronger. I was ready to be
alone, not without support from friends and church, but able to
sleep without fear and to go to work and not come home and cry.

One afternoon when I got home from work, the owner of the
house asked me if I wanted to learn how to cut roses. He and his
wife had an enormous rose garden. He carefully showed me how

to count the leaves from the rose head to know where to cut. Then he told me I was God's princess and all the roses I wanted to cut were mine to enjoy.

I was still feeling damaged and tired, yet he was calling me God's princess. How do you receive something like that?

He left me in the rose garden. As I sat in the sun, I talked to God about the new stage of healing I felt myself entering. Surrounded by roses that afternoon, it felt like my heart was no longer in a dungeon. And yet it was not quite free.

Have you ever been in one place and then a couple of years later find yourself in another place that you never knew existed? Soon after the rape, the picture of my heart was a dungeon full of darkness. Then my healing became like a slow, progressive climb to the light. Where was I now? A picture of a garden, a grate and a tunnel came to mind.

I wonder if you recognize this place?

*U*nderneath a beautiful garden is a tunnel with stairs leading to the surface. I know them well. They lead from the dungeon of my ravaged heart to freedom and light.

Each stair step I had already climbed was another step out of the intensity of my pain. Each muscle that strained and each drop of sweat reminded me of how much work it had taken to keep moving. At the last step, I looked up—only to see an iron grate too heavy to lift. It was keeping me from surfacing out of the darkness.

What was the iron grate? Why did it keep me back from the light and from the freedom I so desired? I tried to budge the grate. I pushed with all my strength, but the bars were too solid. My fingers grasped the iron and, with purple knuckles straining against the bars, I screamed. Had all the climbing been for nothing? Had my hope been in vain?

On the surface walked a man. I could hear the leaves crackle under His feet. He was a stranger to me. My heart was tempted to call out to Him for help, but fear kept me silent. I settled back on the top step, still below the grate. What if He wasn't safe?

As time passed, I realized life on the other side of the grate was continuously changing. The warm weather brought longer days. Birds spoke in languages of praise; flowers sacrificed their fragrance so that I might experience their beauty from underground; and the man continued to walk through the garden. He tended to its needs. This place was His home. Clearly He was the keeper of the garden.

There was always something to uproot and something more to plant. I felt the ground strain as He pulled up roots planted long ago. I heard the shovel pierce the dirt as He prepared a new home for more life. The keeper's changes often made me squirm with discomfort. Yet I could not dismiss how much He seemed to love the place above. He uprooted life, planted life and enjoyed life's beauty at the end of the day. He called each bloom by name.

Though I sat under the grate, my skin felt the kisses of the sun. My eyes sometimes tired from its glare. When it rained, my body felt the dew. At times I could almost imagine I was living above ground, but I was not.

At first I believed the grate kept me from surfacing to the garden. But I began to realize it was not something outside of myself that held me underground. My doubt kept me there. Years after the rape, I found myself sitting under the grate, watching the keeper through the iron bars as He cared for the garden that is me.

Then I heard God whisper to my heart, "There is more. Ignore your doubts and lift up the iron grate." I was paralyzed. My definition of "more" was different from God's definition. I wanted "more" to mean no more pain, suffering, grief or loss. But the garden I saw on the other side of the grate was a place of continuous change and growth. I feared that experiencing life more freely could threaten my hard-won safety.

Seasons change; it isn't summer forever. But then, winter doesn't stay forever either. Beautiful blossoms are pruned away to make room for new life, and old flowers are replaced with new roots. It seems that growth involves change and risking pain. I wanted to avoid pain at all costs.

I sat with this question: Is the keeper of this garden worthy of my trust? I had come to realize He had owned my garden from the beginning. To now want ownership of it for myself, I under-stood to be foolish; I wouldn't know the first thing about the best way to take care of such a beautiful place. That is why He is the keeper of the garden. But could I handle not trying to be in control? I doubted if trust like that was possible.

What a sad picture: my God, the keeper, coming to the grate and asking me to join Him in this beautiful garden, and I couldn't even answer because my reasoning filled with doubt was not His language. He turned and continued to tend the garden, all the time waiting and hoping that I would risk a little more. Every step up the stairs had been a choice and a risk. Lifting the iron grate was one more risk. Would I dare choose to surface from underground and embrace the freedom to change and grow, even with its risks?

Life can seem like a constant warfare between wanting to embrace the hope the keeper gives in abundance and fearing the risk of trusting again.

Some days I would watch myself beginning to crawl toward freedom above ground. I would even sit in the sun with the keeper. But then something pulled me back. The moment I realized that above ground was where I wanted to be and this love with the keeper was what I wanted to know, my heart retreated again. I was afraid to embrace the keeper's intimate love wholeheartedly. I was more content to live in familiar shadows under the iron grate.

The keeper continued to wait.

I couldn't forget His care. When the stairs looked endless, the voice never stopped reminding me that there was something more. I couldn't see what lay beyond the next step, yet the voice pulled me upward. Now, deep inside me, something believed there was more. While I couldn't understand a fulfilling life in a garden where the risk of pain existed side by side with love, I recognized the voice of my keeper as one of goodness to me.

How could I not move on?

Do you ever have a good day, not a perfect day, but a good day; and you think life couldn't possibly be better? That is what life is like below the grate. Only the people who have been through pain would understand this reasoning. When life has been black and incredibly hopeless for so long, you're thankful for whatever light reaches you. Even if you're sitting under a grate, you still feel the sun's warmth, and life doesn't feel nearly as bad as it did. Living fully might be worse.

Wouldn't it be wonderful if being raped qualified us to be exempt from any other trauma and pain in life? I wish that were true. I often think that the people I meet believe it's true. No one wants to admit that freedom doesn't mean exemption from pain.

Freedom means that, yes, you will survive the pain. And when it comes again, yes, you will survive it again. Freedom is being able to push past doubts and open the iron grate that keeps us prisoners in a place that isn't too bad but doesn't help us grow and thrive.

Do you recognize this place? If so, I pray that you are also hearing the keeper's voice and trusting it enough to move you into greater freedom, in spite of the risks involved.

Chapter Ten

Why Forgive?

———

A woman who has been raped does not ask whether a man
bad enough to rape one hundred women is forgivable. She asks
whether she can forgive the man who raped her.

LEWIS B. SMEDES, *FORGIVE AND FORGET:*
HEALING THE HURTS WE DON'T DESERVE

There was a movie playing in the theaters that was a box-office hit. I planned to avoid it at all costs. But when I heard from a reliable Christian source that *Dead Man Walking* was a movie worth seeing, I decided to pray about it. Other friends were talking about how powerful it was, and even a pastor on the radio said that every Christian should see it. I finally decided I would go, but I would also let myself walk out at any point if I felt uncomfortable.

I had heard of the movie's intensity but had no idea what I was in for. The story held my complete attention, and there were a number of scenes that unexpectedly touched my heart. However, there was one scene that screamed out to me as if it were trying to tell me something.

Toward the end of the film, Sean Penn, who plays the convicted rapist, has one last moment to say a few words before he dies. With heaving gasps and burning tears reddening his face, he looks directly at the parents of the victim and says the words they never dreamed he would say. I felt my own body scoot forward in the chair. I wanted to hear him admit to his crime. Isn't that all we ever wanted—to have the perpetrator admit that what he did was wrong? No excuses, just wrong.

And now what the parents and I had wanted was here. The rapist finally admitted to raping the parents' daughter. He asked for forgiveness. In that moment, he was forgiven by a God I don't always understand. He was changed. However, I felt the same.

My eyes shifted to the parents on the screen. Was there evidence that his admission had changed anything for them? No. They were like me. The pain had not lessened; the memories were still bitter and cold. The very words I thought would help me to move on had no power to help them.

I remember feeling very disturbed as I walked out of the theater. I got in the car and began to cry. Disappointment weighed my head down as I tried to fight back the flood of tears. How could I actually have thought the admission of wrongdoing would make everything better?

Then I realized what it meant for me to move on. It meant accepting the realization that if the man who had raped me stood before me right now and begged my forgiveness, it would not bring me freedom. It would definitely be helpful, but it would not repair my heart and make it new again. I would still have the memories and everything they entailed. I had to die to my fantasies of what constituted healing and once again cling to God.

I am not saying it doesn't mean anything when someone asks for forgiveness. Forgiveness is powerful. And I know that when Sean Penn's character asked the parents to forgive him, something happened in the heavenly realms that neither you nor I could see or understand. Yet it is misleading to found all hope of being set free and healed upon a person's words of repentance.

With clenched fists, I had been holding on to the hope that one day, the man who had changed my life forever by his selfish act would feel remorse and that his remorse would make my life all better. I had thought that his confession of guilt would be the day I forgave the crime and moved on. But I realized that forgiveness was not dependent on his remorse. Forgiveness was my choice and it was for me. I would forgive for my sake.

When there is forgiveness, there is a chance to move forward. Does this mean that one afternoon when it's easier to cry than on other days, we sit down and tell God that we forgive the men who hurt us? Yes . . . maybe. Is that the last time we'll ever have to forgive them? No. It surely hasn't been for me.

The other night I used the restroom at a grocery store. It was located in the back of the store. I had to walk through double doors, around boxes of stacked food, through another door, down some stairs, down another hallway and around a corner. As I walked downstairs, all I could hear was a radio playing and a man yelling at one end of the bottom floor. I couldn't see him and I began to wonder if he could see me. What if something happened? Would anyone be able to help me? Would anyone hear me over the blaring radio, through the floor and beyond two sets of doors where I'd left my friends? My mind confirmed it. It was a perfect set-up. I was going to be raped. I knew I had a choice. I could either go back up the stairs and use the restroom when I got home, or I could go forward and fight off my fears.

Sometimes there is a warning in our spirits and we know that God is speaking to our hearts. He can give us discernment to know when we're in a dangerous situation. At other times, fear tries to immobilize us. My sense of boundaries had become strong, and I knew I didn't have to prove anything to myself. But I also had chosen not to live in fear. My sense of this situation did not seem like a warning to avoid going down the stairs; it just felt like pure fear.

I continued on, found the restroom and tried not to run back up to the main floor, lest someone think there was something the matter. I was proud of myself for not running. But a little deeper inside me I was angry that I had even felt scared. It was time to forgive the man who had hurt me. Again.

These little unexpected challenges come up every so often and more than I prefer. It's like being in a boat when you feel the wind pick up and watch the whitecaps form. The waves cause you to feel jostled and out of control. Water slaps the side of your boat and you realize your peace is quickly leaving. You are afraid.

Do you remember the disciples in the boat with Jesus while He slept? Before they knew it, they were in a full-fledged storm. And Jesus just slept. How could He do that? Do you blame the disciples for waking Him up? Wouldn't you have been terrified? All the evidence you needed to fear for your life was white-capped and taller than your boat. So why did Jesus think His disciples were irrational? Why did He practically scold them for their fear? I believe it's because when they first got in the boat, He had announced to them all, "We're going to the other side."

I can hear His Spirit say it to me now. "We're going to the other side, Me Ra. Don't let the fierce waves misguide your hope. Don't let the roar of thunder discount what I've said. I am faithful to My promises; today I promise that you will see the other side and you will touch land."

We live for the days when the storms subside. There is a voice that tries to tell us that a lack of storms in our lives is evidence of wholeness. As much as those words tickle my ears, I keep hearing this "annoying" promise of Jesus: You *will* see troubles in this lifetime, but do not fear. I am with you (see John 16:33). Storms—occurrences promised by God. Are they also disguised grace? Some storms are tragic and some are fierce. But all have a beginning and an end.

I am thinking about the storms present in my life right now. A majority of them have nothing to do with the rape or with my friend's suicide. Some of my storms are because of uncontrollable circumstances; some are from others' hurtful words or actions. And then there are the storms that rage from within myself.

It is important to hold on to truth in the midst of the storms, because their presence or absence does not measure our degree of healing. There are simply bad days from which no one can escape. And sometimes there are bad weeks.

When a storm comes because of some painful or frightening reminder of the rape, I must remind myself that it cannot disrupt my healing. If I am obedient to forgive—as many times as I need to—I will find healing. If I trust that God has the ability to heal the impossible situation, I will find healing. If I take one day at a time and thank God for all the things He has given me, I will find healing.

Because God is love in the midst of our obedience, trust and praise, miracles of healing live.

Chapter Eleven

A Vision of Brides

———

*"You were thrown out into the open field, when you yourself were
loathed. . . . And when I passed by you and saw you struggling in your own
blood, I said to you in your blood, 'Live!' Yes, I said to you in your blood,
'Live!' . . . but you were naked and bare. When I passed by you again and
looked upon you, indeed your time was the time of love; so I spread My wing
over you and covered your nakedness. Yes, I swore an oath to you and
entered into a covenant with you, and you became Mine," says the Lord
GOD. "Then I washed you in water; yes, I thoroughly washed off your blood,
and I anointed you with oil. I clothed you in embroidered cloth and gave you
sandals . . . fine linen . . . silk. . . . And I put a . . . beautiful crown on your
head. . . . You were exceedingly beautiful, and succeeded to royalty. Your
fame went out among the nations because of your beauty, for it was perfect
through My splendor which I had bestowed on you," says the Lord GOD.*

EZEKIEL 16:5-14, NKJV

When I first began this journey of healing, I felt like the woman
in Ezekiel 16. I felt as if I had been thrown into an open field, left
alone, exposed for all to see and surrounded by my own blood.
As I lay there in my shame, I watched the Lord come into my
dark wilderness and speak life into my spirit. I felt Him cover
my nakedness and slowly deliver me from my pain. He replaced
my ragged clothes with His royal wardrobe.

How did I see this? God used my mom and my friends Emma,
Lynne and Taylor to love me back to life. He used the women I

worked with in the catering business. He also used the older couple who let me move in with them and share their roses, and He used my church.

Even though I have not mentioned it much, it's important for you to know how much the church helped to bring healing into my life. For over two years, almost every Sunday morning and Sunday night, I would go up for prayer at the end of the service. It didn't matter what the focus of the sermon was; if prayer for needs was offered, I went up for more prayer.

Usually, I would kneel at the front of the sanctuary and cry. Women would pass by me and often pray for God's healing. Whether or not my mind heard every prayer, my spirit received the truths they were praying.

I will never forget one particular night when the pastor's wife prayed for me. With her soft, gentle voice she said, "God, I pray that You would show Me Ra how You are like a dawn rising within her heart."

I sat in silence, picturing what that might look like. As I listened, God unfolded a beautiful promise to me that I believe is for all of us.

Spread out before me was a grassy field edged by the black outline of a mountain range in the distance. The cold morning air prickled my skin as dawn began to peek over the mountains. Already the color of the sky was changing from violet purple to sporadic streaks of crimson red. Its beauty captivated me. My heart felt pulled toward the light, and I began walking forward.

As I got closer to the light of the dawn, it revealed my clothing. I was dressed like a precious bride. My gown was of the finest linen and embroidered cloth. I touched my hair and felt small flowers and golden twine braided through it. My body had been bathed in rich fragrances. On my wedding finger was a gold ring. On my head I wore a crown of jewels. The wind rose up around me; and I heard the whisper of a calm voice say, "Because of the Lord's splendor, your beauty has been made perfect, declares your Sovereign Lord." I felt myself smile as the sun's warmth kissed my face. I was beautiful. I was a bride.

Out of the corner of my eye, I saw women hiding in the shadows behind trees, bushes and boulders. My instinct was to turn and call them out to join me. But the calm voice invited me to continue forward. I could not forget about the women. My heart cried out, "What if the women don't follow the dawn's light? They won't know they are also brides of this light!"

Then I heard the rustle of clothing behind me. Women from all parts of the field were coming out of the shadows and joining me on the path toward the light. They, too, were radiant with beauty. As each one stepped closer and closer to the light, the whiteness of her dress shone brighter. I looked at the women's faces and saw that the radiant light that brought warmth to me was now touching each of them. Light was seeping into every hidden place.

The vision of the rising dawn is a vital picture to me as I go forward in my own healing and as I continue to long for yours. The picture reminded me that the coming of a new day is not dependent on our own strength. It is the dawn's light that captivates. I did not walk toward it because I thought it was the right thing to do. The beauty of God's love called me forward even while I was still in the darkness of night.

God wanted me to know that in His light, I can see myself and you can see yourself as He sees us: beautiful, clean, whole. It isn't our beauty or achievements or freedom from pain that causes us to be so; it is the Lord's great love that restores us by freeing and perfecting His beauty in us.

Just as the dawn's rising has nothing to do with my strength but everything to do with God's grace, I know that it isn't my persuasion or encouragement that will bring you to freedom. It will always be the grace of God's love. He longs for freedom to reign in all of us. He wants us to stand with confidence and no longer fear tomorrow. Each of our paths will be different; no experience of pain or healing is exactly like someone else's. But in Him, we are all led to freedom.

How wonderful to know that no matter what fears we might battle or what pain we might suffer, there is still a dawn rising within our hearts! It is based on the promise of God's continual work in our lives, which brings a type of healing we could not hope for without Him.

I take comfort in knowing that I'm not in control. I can only do as much as I can, and the rest is up to God's timing. I cannot slow the sunrise or speed it up. It simply awakens at God's desire. Even as I wait for the night to end, all I am asked to do is walk toward the light as a new dawn is born.

The support of friends and family is vital to our healing. The loving arms of a praying church cannot be overestimated. Although a job or an education can help us learn how to carry responsibility again, nothing compares to the hope we are given in God's love for us. If all other things fail on our journey to healing, we can rest assured that when we tell Him all about our feelings and needs, His love will find a way to grow within us, eventually bringing light into every hidden corner of our hearts.

Thank You, Jesus.

Chapter Twelve

Eight Years After the Rape

—

To live with fear and not to be afraid is the final test of maturity.

EDWARD WEEKS, *BETTER THAN GOD*

I did not date much during my last years of college and as I went on to graduate school. Instead I developed strong friendships. Three men in particular were determined to show me that all men were not like the one who had taken advantage of me. They became like brothers to me in the safety of our church and the company of other friends.

Then one day, I met Brian. We went to the same church; but the ironic part of it is that our grandparents had been best friends for over 40 years. We just had to be friends; there was no question about it.

Two things in particular struck me about Brian: He loved to laugh (so did I), and he often referred to my girlfriends and me as "ladies." He was the only man I knew who still called women ladies. Whenever he would refer to me that way, I could feel my self-worth grow and my femininity blossom. After three years of a wonderful friendship, which grew into love, Brian and I were married.

Before and after our wedding, we spent months in counseling, preparing for all the different ways the rape might affect us. Our counselor taught us what to do if I had a flashback when we were being sexually intimate. He taught Brian to hold me, to remind me of where I was and of who he was, and then just to sit with me until I came back from wherever the flashback had taken me.

There were many nights during our first two years of marriage when I would have a flashback and Brian would say, "Me Ra, you're safe. We're in our home. I'm your husband, Brian, and I am here to protect you. It's 11:30 at night. I'm just going to wait until my precious wife comes back. I'm just going to wait here for you." And then he would pray.

The gentleness of his words and the patience of his spirit have brought deeper levels of healing to the rape. It is a sacrifice when he shifts from being an intimate partner to the role of husband-protector; but after two years of marriage, the flashbacks come less and less and we believe that one day they will not come at all.

Brian and I have often talked about what we will someday share with our children about my past. We have decided that when they're mature enough, we will share the whole story with them. We will work at talking about our sexuality with them in healthy ways, instead of ignoring the issue. We want our children to grow up free from the shame I once carried and wise about what makes a person susceptible to false love.

For now, my husband and I take one day at a time. We both prepare ourselves for the emotions that rise in me the week before Valentine's Day. It's amazing how my spirit will grieve the rape before I even realize that Valentine's Day is a week away. Brian has learned to let me grieve during the day, but he also makes sure the day ends with a new memory of love—real love.

For the most part, I rarely think about the rape anymore. But every once in a while, I will see someone who looks like the man who raped me and I'll feel my stomach drop. Or I'll go in for my annual physical and will cry through my pap exam, fighting so hard to keep the memory of the rape away. I usually experience these moments of life alone. And no matter how supportive my husband, family, friends and church have been, I can still feel alone. Yet the loneliness changes.

I like to say it this way: I can still hit bottom at times, but the bottom has been raised. I have this sneaky suspicion that when I'm feeling good and living on top of the ground, God runs over to my pit of despair and starts filling it up with dirt. Whenever I get discouraged and feel myself start to sink, I'm always amazed that my pit of despair isn't as deep as it once was. I call this God's mercy—and what a beautiful thing it is.

My prayer is that while you have been reading this book, God has been playing the same sneaky trick on you. I have confidence in the Lord's ability to heal your heart. He promised us a life that is *full*. Maybe your heart can't believe that right now. Dear sister, don't worry about believing. Just rest. I know the Lord will find you.

Appendix One

How Others Viewed
My Journey to Healing

Through the Eyes of a Close Friend

—

BY LYNNE SCHERRER

Sleepless nights, empty stares, silence broken again and again by heart-wrenching cries—these are the images that immediately come to mind as I reflect on the state of my dear friend Me Ra during the early days of her journey toward healing. The days seemed like months; the months like years. What had happened to the Me Ra I knew? Her infectious laughter was now silent, and the smile that had graced her face and blessed our hearts was no more. She felt no hope—only darkness.

What could I do during those many times I heard her cries and came to her bedside, sometimes when she and I were the only ones at home? Many times I would come home to find her just sitting there quietly. My heart ached to know how to help.

What could I say? Those of us who have walked alongside someone during their difficult time know that there is great pain in not knowing what to do.

When I look back at my experiences in life, I've had to learn that there are many things I can't fix. Instead, I must rely on the Holy Spirit's leading, and trust that God's hand covers those who are in despair. The following verse summarizes my deepest prayer during times like these. This verse was spoken prophetically of the Lord Jesus, but it is also something we can ask God's Spirit to work in us.

The Lord GOD has given Me the tongue of the learned, that I should know how to speak a word in season to him who is weary. He awakens Me morning by morning, he awakens My ear to hear as the learned (Isa. 50:4, *NKJV*).

God is the One who provides the strength and wisdom to speak words of life to the hurting. As we spend time in prayer, earnestly listening and seeking His voice, He is faithful to work through us. Many times when I went to encourage Me Ra, I had no idea what I was going to say. Even while walking over to her, I would cry out to God for guidance. He welcomes those kinds of prayers, because He desires a humble heart that seeks His help. He promises that "[His] strength is made perfect in weakness" (2 Cor. 12:9, *NKJV*).

So often my heart's prayer was *Please, God, speak for me when I have no words or am unsure of how to word the few that I have. Please, Holy Spirit, provide me with wisdom that knows when to just sit in silence and speak not a word. Please, Lord, let me find those Scriptures that are meant just for her. And please, Lord, give me the strength to say Your words of truth, even though they might not be well received.*

My heart desperately wanted to make the pain go away, yet it also knew that I must rely on God and leave it in His hands. In those times when I didn't know what to do, I learned that I could always offer hope and unconditional love—the love Jesus modeled perfectly and gives us freely.

By His grace, we can extend a love that listens without judging, and we can willingly give up time and a busy agenda to just sit with a friend, even if it means sitting in silence. When we fail to do this well, we must remember that God still has His hand on our friend's life. No matter how imperfect our delivery of comfort, a hurting friend knows when she is truly being loved.

Sometimes we must give a friend hope when she can't grasp it for herself. To do that, we must stay rooted in God's Word and keep our own faith strong by depending on the God who is faithful to fulfill His promises. Here are just a couple of His promises to the hurting:

> [He will] give them beauty for ashes, the oil of joy for mourning, the garment of praise for the spirit of heaviness (Isa. 61:3, *NKJV*).

> Behold, I will do a new thing, now it shall spring forth. Shall you not know it? I will even make a road in the wilderness and rivers in the desert. . . . I will make darkness light before them (Isa. 43:19; 42:16, *NKJV*).

When a friend is hurting, remind her often of the light at the end of the tunnel. Point it out. Tell her that even though she can't see it at the moment, she will see it one day.

Now when I look at Me Ra, my heart cannot help but rejoice to see that God's precious promises have finally come to fruition in her life. Because I walked alongside her through her dark valley, my life has been thoroughly enriched and there is a special bond between us. It is beautiful to see the truth of this Scripture in Me Ra's life: "So the ransomed of the LORD shall return, and come to Zion with singing, with everlasting joy on their head. They shall obtain joy and gladness; sorrow and sighing shall flee away"(Isa. 51:11, *NKJV*).

Yes, sorrows still come, but Me Ra can now see, believe and rest in that beautiful hope.

Through a Mother's Eyes

BY CHERRI LEE

The courtroom. My daughter is standing alone before a judge with no one to protect her, no one to fight for her. He's there too, just a few feet away. She won't let me into her pain. So I sit. From here I can only see her back, yet every gesture speaks to me. He brought a lawyer, and they are tearing away at my daughter's soul as the sickening memory of that night is repeated one more time. A decision is made. There will be no restraining order, no way to keep him off campus or away from her. I want to scream at the injustice, but who would hear?

. . . .

Me Ra's phone call. Her voice seemed to fade as the words pierced my heart and the pain swept through me. I think back to that moment. Was I compassionate? Did she hear my heart crying out to her? Were my words filled with love and support? Should I have said less? Could I have said more? All I remember now is hanging up the phone and sinking to the floor.

No, no, Lord! Not my little girl! Why, Lord, why? I tried so hard to protect her. No one had escaped my watchful eyes. I trusted You. Lord, You were supposed to take care of her while she was away at college. I prayed for her protection every day. Where were You?

I'm not sure how long I sat there crying. Even after the tears had stopped, the pain continued. There would be more tears; they would come suddenly when the pain in her voice replayed in my mind.

What do I hear, Lord? Her shame? My guilt?

Voices condemned without a spoken word—voices that stayed with me every night. The nights were so long, and I would find myself on the floor of our dining room, exhausted from crying. I was crying out to God for my little girl to have the strength to just hold on for one more day. Where would her healing come from? I knew that without the Lord's strength and constant, gentle love, she would not survive.

Thank You for never leaving us, Lord.

. . . .

A new battle begins. I tell myself that I must be strong to help Me Ra win this war. What we are fighting and the identity of our enemy will change many times over the next several years. As a mom, I have always rushed in to try and solve my children's problems. Now I must be here to support my daughter and allow her to lead.

For all that I have to learn, Me Ra becomes my teacher. My heart hurts over the smallest of things, like when I try to reach out and hold her and she pulls away. Learning her needs and knowing when to offer comfort take a great amount of effort. It means putting my needs and feelings aside. I must accept her constant mood swings; her irritability cannot be taken personally.

There is so much anger that we must allow ourselves to own and express I know that Jesus understands the anger. But anger was the feeling I had always denied and not allowed my children to freely express. I would now begin the long, hard process of learning to express my feelings and my own pain locked away inside my heart.

. . . .

Where was everyone? Why hadn't anyone rushed in to join our battle? It still seems impossible to understand and accept that there was not the support I expected from loved ones. It was almost as if they couldn't understand or feel the outrage of being raped. At times I felt very much alone, without anyone to share my pain. Bitterness and resentment began to take root in my heart as loved ones failed to live up to my expectations.

Did they not see Me Ra sinking from the pain? If they could only have looked into her eyes, her heart would have revealed so much. We both felt isolated and alone. Unspoken words felt like condemnation: "You should have known better. You should not have been there with that guy. Didn't you see what kind of person he was? We tried to tell you."

How easy it is to judge others when you are suffering.

"Rape," a word that most of us could not even force ourselves to say, now became a part of our daily conversation. So many misconceptions attached to this single act of violence give it power to destroy and violate. Now I know that the important thing to do for someone who is experiencing a personal crisis is just to love them—to love them with all that you know love to be.

You don't have to have the right words—just let them know you care. Let them know their pain has not been forgotten.

It is so very important to declare to your children your unconditional love. They must know beyond any doubt that you believe in them and are willing to stand beside them, whatever the cost. Sometimes when you choose to support a child in need, you will also risk other relationships. It is not easy to know that your relationships within the family may suffer, because your energy is being focused on the one in crisis.

In our family, a certain amount of chaos broke loose and all of our relationships suddenly needed attention. We all sensed the strain of adjusting as Me Ra and I had begun to change. Growth and healing through difficult times always change who we are and how we relate to others. Sometimes this threatens our family members. They may have preferred the "old mom" or the "old sister." Lots of love and attention must be given to reassure everyone that they, too, are loved and important. It can be an exhausting ordeal.

I now realize, at a deeper level, the difficult tasks of being a mother. We seem to always give, while much of the time our own tanks run on empty. I could never make it without Jesus filling me up. I have relearned the importance of constantly going to Him to be renewed. I will always be striving to learn how to make Christ the source of my strength—during the smallest and the biggest ordeals. When I lay my head on His lap, He strokes my hair and speaks to my childlike heart of His love. I will make it through another day and so will Me Ra.

The year following the rape seemed to pass so slowly. Me Ra struggled to remain in school and function normally. What is normal anyway?

Late one night I received a call from Me Ra. She needed help. Stephen Arterburn was on campus and had spoken about New

Life Clinics. His words of hope and healing must have pierced Me Ra's heart. She was found later that day on the floor of her dormitory room, lying in a fetal position, crying. She had been that way for several hours. When they spoke to her, her voice was that of a scared little girl's. A friend told her that it was time to get serious help—now.

Was New Life an option? Mr. Arterburn was someone she felt she could trust. Her strength to fight the battle was quickly dying. She could no longer fight alone. Her father and I talked. But how could we know if this place could help Me Ra? How would we pay for it? So many uncertainties, yet Me Ra needed help now. Somehow the Lord would have to provide as we stepped out in faith.

Later, a counselor referred to Me Ra's condition as an emotional heart attack. If someone you loved had had a heart attack, you wouldn't decide to get help based on whether you had insurance or could afford a clinic. You would seek emergency help immediately! The same is true of an emotional heart attack. You would find a qualified person who specialized in victim abuse and take part in a program of counseling until healing and restoration had come full circle.

It may take several years of counseling to work through all the issues related to rape. It is extremely important to encourage your child to seek help and deal with the pain. Shame will try to tell you that everything should be okay by now; enough time has passed and everyone should get on with their lives, right? No. That is a lie. Don't allow that lie to become truth while your child is suffering inside. A child is so fragile and usually feels that he or she is carrying the burden alone. Guilt can quickly translate into depression and suicide. Me Ra was like a beautiful crystal vase that had been shattered.

. . . .

Standing there at the airport, I struggle to hold back my tears. I watch as Me Ra gets on a plane that will take her to a hospital far away from me. The weeks to follow will be the most difficult time of her life. I am so proud of the woman who is choosing to face her fears, to deal with them now and not 20 or 30 years from now.

So many of us have buried our pain and slammed the doors shut. We become fearful, perfectionistic, unable to trust and have a need to be in control. At that moment, Me Ra became one of the most courageous women I know.

As I drove home, my stomach felt sick as I cried for the little girl who had done nothing wrong. Life is so unfair. Why must our children suffer so much pain? *Lord, protect and watch over her,* I prayed. *Please give her courage and strength. Help Me Ra to know that she is not alone. Help me, too, Lord. Tomorrow is another day.*

. . . .

As I write this, it has been four years since Me Ra was at the New Life Clinic. Our family can see how much healing the Lord has brought to every part of her life. The rape brought death to so much of who Me Ra was, yet the Lord has brought from it new life. Every member of our family has been changed; we are no longer the same people we used to be.

God is so faithful! He has brought incredible healing to all of our lives. He has taught us how to share our feelings with each other and how to speak the truth in love. Being real is not always easy and not everyone will always be pleased with us. But it is the way our Lord tells us we should love each other; we must learn how to confront and seek the best for each other—no more pretending; no more manipulating; no more power playing or trying to control. This new, real love brought all things into order.

We now have a shared respect for each other. It has been more than I could have asked of the Lord.

Is it possible to be thankful or to praise the Lord for the rape? *Dare I even whisper such sacrifice of praise to You, Lord? My tears flow from the depth of the pain and from the even greater depth of Your love.*

Appendix Two

Resources for Rape Victims and Those Who Want to Help Them

The Legal Definition of Rape

Each state varies in its exact legal definition of rape. Even so, I believe it is important to have a general idea of the definition as a starting point for understanding and action. Due to unawareness or lack of education about date rape, most women do not realize that certain harmful acts are legally unacceptable. If you think that your boyfriend or someone else has crossed a physical boundary with you, I encourage you to call a local college, ask for the law school and then ask for your state's legal definition of rape.

The following is a brief summary of the rape law in Washington State:

> Forcible sexual intercourse without the person's consent. Sexual intercourse means penetration, however slight, with a penis or an object (such as a finger or pencil), either vaginally or anally. This definition also covers forced oral sex. Offender and victim may be of same or opposite sex.

The purpose for encouraging you to know the legal definition of rape is to help you become more aware of what has happened to you so that you can continue your road to healing. Before we can come to a place of complete healing, we must first be able to admit and talk about what really happened to us. Date rape will always be one of the most confusing crimes to talk about. Yet if you have been hurt, no matter how confusing your situation might have been, it is important for you to talk to someone and be able to clearly understand which boundaries it is always inappropriate to violate.

Please also remember that anything said of date rape also applies to acquaintance rape. Being violated by someone you thought of as a friend you could trust is no different from being violated by someone with whom you're out on an "official" date.

Rape Statistics

"Rape" is often a taboo word we do not like to speak aloud. However, it is a real issue in our society. The purpose of sharing these statistics is to increase awareness of the severity of the rape epidemic.

- In a 1992 study conducted by the Crime Victims Research and Treatment Center, it was found that only 22 percent of rape victims were assaulted by someone they had never seen before or did not know well; 9 percent were raped by husbands or ex-husbands; 11 percent by their fathers or stepfathers; 10 percent by boyfriends or ex-boyfriends; 16 percent by other relatives; 29 percent by other nonrelatives, such as friends and neighbors.[1]

- Acccording to a National Crime Victimization Survey (NCVS), there were 171,420 rapes reported in 1991. That is 469 rapes each day of the year, or 19 each hour, or 1 rape every 3.5 minutes.[2]

- Of the rapes reported to NCVS between 1987-1991, intimates (husbands, ex-spouses, boyfriends, ex-boyfriends) committed 20 percent, acquaintances committed 50 percent and strangers committed 30 percent.[3]

- About 16,000 women a year have abortions as a result of rape or incest.[4]

- Only 1 in 100 rapists is sentenced to more than one year in prison.[5]

- One study revealed that during a 20-year period, as many as 12 million women and children—nearly 10 percent of the current female population of the United States—had been raped.[6]

- One in four college women have been or will be the victim of rape or attempted rape.[7]

Notes

1. National Victim Center and the Crime Victims Research and Treatment Center, *Rape in America: A Report to the Nation* (April 23, 1992), pp. 1-16, quoted in Emilie Buchwald, Pamela R. Fletcher, Martha Roth, eds., *Transforming a Rape Culture* (Minneapolis: Milkweed Editions, 1993), p. 9. The National Women's Study (NWS), issued in 1992, was conducted by the Crime Victims Research and Treatment Center. The respondents were women 18 years and older at the time of the intitial survey.
2. United States Department of Justice, *National Crime Victimization Survey Report: Criminal Victimization in the United States, 1991* (December 1992), pp. 72-75, 79, 148, 149, NCJ-1399563; and Caroline Wolf Jarlow, *Female Victims of Violent Crime* (January 1991), pp. 1-3, 7, NCJ-126826.
3. Ibid.
4. The Alan Guttmacher Institute, "Facts in Brief: Abortion in the United States" (1993), p. 1. These are 1991 statistics of the National Committee for Prevention of Child Abuse.
5. The Majority Staff of the Senate Judiciary Committee, "The Response to Rape: Detours on the Road to Equal Justice" (May 1993), pp. 1, 25-60. These are 1991 statistics of the National Committee for Prevention of Child Abuse.
6. Emilie Buchwald, Pamela R. Fletcher and Martha Roth, eds., *Transforming a Rape Culture* (Minneapolis: Milkweed Editions, 1993), p. 9.
7. Robin Warshaw, *I Never Called It Rape: The M.S. Report on Recognizing, Fighting, and Surviving Date Rape and Acquaintance Rape* (New York: Harper Collins, 1994), n.p.

Characteristics of Date/Acquaintance Rapists*

Although there is no profile of a typical date or acquaintance rapist, experts have identified behavioral characteristics that tend to be exhibited by date and acquaintance rapists. Awareness of these characteristics, listed below, may help you to identify these people.

- Acts immaturely; shows little empathy or feeling for others and displays little social conscience
- Displays anger or aggression, either physically or verbally (The anger need not be directed toward you but may be displayed during conversations by general negative references to women, vulgarity, curtness toward others, and the like. Women are often viewed as adversaries.)
- Behaves in a macho manner and discusses acts of physical prowess
- Displays a short temper; slaps and/or twists arms
- Acts excessively jealous and/or possessive (Be especially suspicious of this behavior if you have recently met the person or are on a first or second date.)
- Ignores your space boundaries by coming too close or placing his hand on your thigh, etc. (Be particularly cognizant of this behavior when it is displayed in public.)
- Ignores your wishes
- Attempts to make you feel guilty or accuses you of being uptight
- Becomes hostile and/or increasingly more aggressive when you say no
- Acts particularly friendly at a party or bar and tries to separate you from your friends

- Insists on being alone with you on a first date
- Demands your attention or compliance at inappropriate times, such as during class
- Asks personal questions and is interested in knowing more about you than you want to tell him
- Subscribes excessively to traditional male and female stereotypes

If you are with a person who exhibits the kind of behavior described above, be very cautious and take your time in getting to know the person. Work on being a skilled listener who is aware of remarks and comments that may reveal true feelings.

Many date and acquaintance rapists plan for the rape and then set out to find the victim. They often test a potential victim. For example, such a rapist may try placing a hand on a potential victim's thigh. If she does not react, even if she obviously feels uncomfortable, the rapist identifies her as easy prey.

A date rapist often tries to get a potential victim to trust him and then invents some reason for her to come to his residence. The date rapist is usually very manipulative and tries to con an unsuspecting victim.

Many date rapists are repeat offenders and are skilled at identifying weaknesses in potential victims. The rapist is looking for a woman he can control, because his primary motivation is power rather than sex.

Some date rapists exhibit a Jekyll-and-Hyde personality. They may appear to be great guys. But when under stress or when they find a vulnerable victim, their personalities change.

*Adapted from Carol Pritchard, *Avoiding Rape On and Off Campus* (Wenonah, NJ: State College Publishing Company, 1988). Used by permission.

Help Immediately After a Rape*

You can play a vital role in giving help to someone who is raped. That person will need immediate and knowledgeable medical, psychological or legal assistance.

You probably aren't a doctor, psychologist, lawyer or law enforcement officer. But you don't need to be in order to help someone who has been raped. People who have mastered CPR save the lives of thousands of heart attack victims. In a similar way, you can provide the crucial immediate help, emotional support, guidance and direction that a rape victim desperately needs.

If you are giving help to a person who has been raped, or if you are the victim, immediately do the following:

1. Leave the scene of the crime and go to a trusted friend. (Professionals state that a friend is better than a family member because a friend will be somewhat emotionally removed and better able to focus on doing step 2.)
2. Call the police or campus security.
3. Go to the college infirmary or a hospital.
4. Contact a rape crisis center.

Select the quickest option and, if possible, the one that will not require the victim to drive or to walk any distance. It is important that she not delay. Seeking help immediately is critical.

---

*Excerpted from Carol Pritchard, *Avoiding Rape On and Off Campus* (Wenonah, NJ: State College Publishing Company, 1988). Used by permission.

Emergency Numbers and Organizations

If you need help and don't know where to go, or if you have a friend who needs help and you don't know who to call, there are several organizations that may be able to assist you.

Focus on the Family: 1-800-A-FAMILY (8 A.M. to 5 P.M. MST, Monday through Friday). Ask for the counseling department and/or counseling referral line. FOF is a good general resource for tapes, books and counseling referrals. If you would like to talk with a counselor immediately, call 719-531-3400, ext. 2700. An assistant will set up a time for you to speak with a counselor by phone ASAP.

New Life Clinics: 1-800-639-4673 for counseling referrals and book resources; 1-800-NEW LIFE for a 24-hour hot line and connection to their inpatient clinics. New Life provides help through hospital programs, counseling services, radio outreach and resource materials. They are equipped to deal with people who are barely holding on to life. If you or someone you know is struggling to hold on, call New Life and take the first step to getting help.

Rapha Treatment Centers: 1-800-383-4673 (7 A.M. to 10 P.M. EST; a counselor can be paged during off-hours). Provides Christ-centered professional counseling that integrates medical and clinical care with biblically based therapy.

The Center for the Prevention of Sexual and Domestic Violence: 1-206-634-1903; website: http://www.cpsdv.org. This center is an educational nonprofit agency that works with religious communities of all types to address issues of sexual and domestic violence. For information on training or for educational videos and books, call their phone number or visit their website.

Check your telephone directory for rape relief or crisis centers near you.

Rape Trauma Syndrome*

Many rape victims suffer from Rape Trauma Syndrome. Symptoms include loss of appetite, sleep disturbance, nightmares, extreme phobias, preoccupation with the rape, anxiety about leaving the home and being with other people, inability to concentrate on studies and/or work, and sexual dysfunction. Without treatment, these symptoms may last for years.

Dr. Georgia Witkin-Lanoil notes that Rape Trauma Syndrome has three stages:

1. **The acute phase:** In her silence, a woman's emotions may be expressed as physical symptoms: headaches, sleeplessness, nausea, muscle spasms or vaginismus (involuntary contraction of the muscles surrounding the vagina, making intercourse painful or impossible). In addition, she usually experiences confusion, depression, anxiety, nightmares and jumpiness.

2. **The chronic phase:** After several days, a victim of date [or acquaintance] rape seems to slide into preoccupation with her role in the incident and a constant replaying of memories to figure out if she might have prevented it. The alternative is a temporary "adjustment" period that is based on denial of the incident.

3. **The long-term reorganization phase:** Often six or more months must pass before the victim digests and incorporates the reality of the experience. She can no longer avoid the telephone; she must deal with sex; she must seek treatment for residual phobias. Perhaps most important, the victim must acknowledge her anger so that she can move on with

her life, rather than spending energy trying to hide or control that anger.

*Excerpted from Carol Pritchard, *Avoiding Rape On and Off Campus* (Wenonah, NJ: State College Publishing Company, 1988). Used by permission.

Recommended Reading

Arterburn, Stephen F., and Stoop, David A. *When Someone You Love Is Someone You Hate*. Dallas: Word Publishing, 1988. The worst part about date rape can be the fact that you actually had sentimental feelings for the guy. This book discusses that issue and helps the reader break free from unhealthy ties. It does not focus specifically on date rape; instead, it looks at a wide range of love/hate relationships.

Buchwald, Emilie; Fletcher, Pamela; and Roth, Martha. *Transforming a Rape Culture*. Minneapolis: Milkweed Editions, 1993. This is a compilation of information from authors who are victims, activists, educators, theologians, political leaders and members of the general public. The book's content brings awareness of the rape culture in which we are living. This is an excellent resource for a wide range of views on the topic of rape.

Carter, Christine, ed. *The Other Side of Silence: Women Tell About Their Experiences with Date Rape*. Gilsum, New Hampshire: Avocus Publishers, 1997. Health professionals consider the personal accounts of women victimized by date rape and include a state-by-state listing of rape crisis centers. Written from a secular viewpoint, it discusses factors commonly involved in rape situations, methods of recovery and frequently asked questions.

Frank, Jan. *A Door of Hope*. San Bernardino, California: Here's Life Publishers, 1987. This book was recommended to me more than any other. It is the author's personal story of being an incest victim at the age of 10. She shares her wisdom in 10 proven steps to recovery and also invites the reader to hear the stories of others. The book can bring a sense of freedom to those who feel isolated by their pain.

Hansel, Tim. *You Gotta Keep Dancin'*. Elgin, Illinois: David C. Cook Publishing Co., 1985. This is the author's own story of how he found hope after a traumatic accident. Tim Hansel knows what it's like to sit at the bottom of the pit and wonder if you'll ever see light again. His book offers encouragement and generates laughter and tears. He once told me over the phone to take life three minutes at a time. His advice has pulled me through many hopeless hours. A day can feel like a mountain, but three minutes . . . I could always do three minutes. Thanks, Tim Hansel.

Hillerstrom, Roger P. *Intimate Deception*. Portland, Oregon: Multnomah Press, 1989. This book focuses on the power of intimacy in relationships and gives insight on how our hearts deal with love, sex and the need for intimacy. The author's straightforward delivery lessens the reader's focus on guilt and shame and points the way toward getting free from the past.

Hurnard, Hannah. *Hinds' Feet on High Places*. Wheaton, Illinois: Tyndale House Publishers, 1977. This is my favorite! Written in an allegorical style, this book offers a message of hope through the main character, Much-Afraid. Few books have articulated my heart's feelings like this one. If your heart has tasted the word "pain," you will be blessed by reading *Hinds' Feet*.

Jakes, T. D. *Daddy Loves His Girls*. Orlando, Florida: Creation House, 1996. This is a wonderful book for the woman who needs to see how much her Father in heaven adores her. It's sad to admit that we live in a fatherless generation. The author does an amazing job of revealing the Father's love for His little girls and calls women out by reminding them of their gifts and unique beauty. This book will bless you!

Lechman, Judith C. *The Spirituality of Gentleness*. New York: Harper & Row Publishers, 1987. I remember reading this book for a specific reason. My heart knew how to be angry, bitter and sad, but I had forgotten what it looked like to be gentle. I wanted to fall in love with the gentleness of God again. And I wanted people to see God's testimony of healing in my life through the display of gentleness. This book points the way toward growth into the fruit of gentleness.

Payne, Leanne. *The Broken Image*. Westchester, Illinois: Crossway Books, 1981. Countless lives have been affected by Leanne Payne's seminars. If you ever have a chance to attend one, you will be forever changed. *The Broken Image* is just one of her books, but it is touted as a classic and specifically deals with wholeness out of sexual brokenness.

Pritchard, Carol. *Avoiding Rape On and Off Campus*. Wenonah, New Jersey: State College Publishing Company, 1988. This 68-page booklet is written specifically for the environment of a college campus. The information and research provided is educating, insightful and necessary for all college students to know. When I needed facts and straightforward advice, Pritchard's booklet was the best I could find.

Scott, Kay. *Sexual Assault: Will I Ever Feel Okay Again?* Minneapolis, Minnesota: Bethany House Publishers, 1993. This personal testimony of a woman who was raped while working in an inner-city ministry tells how she walked her road to healing. It is an intense book. You will feel the fear, pain, shame and confusion that Kay Scott experienced. You will also feel the hope she found. This book is also a good resource for parents, friends, spouses and pastors who are struggling to know how to help their loved ones.

Warshaw, Robin. *I Never Called It Rape: The M.S. Report on Recognizing, Fighting, and Surviving Date Rape and Acquaintance Rape*. New York: Harper Collins, 1994. This is a compilation of first-person accounts of women who have been date raped. Warshaw does a respectable job of exploring the issues behind date rape and answering such larger questions as, What is date rape? and Why does it happen? She includes a